More Advance Praise for Red-Hot Customers:

Congratulations on your new book! I'm sure it will
help thousands of executives in the sales profession.
My only prayer is that none of my competitors read it.
> —Jeffrey Becker
> Director of Catering
> Hyatt Hotels

> I find that your book provides an excellent real-world,
> customer-focused approach to selling. It is full of great
> information and practical selling tips. *Red-Hot
> Customers* is an excellent selling book for new and
> experienced sales representatives.
>> —Vincent F. Peters
>> Sales Training Director
>> Wyeth-Ayerst Global Pharmaceuticals

Red-Hot Customers is a well-written book with a clear
and coherent message. It offers many valuable insights
and practical strategies for anyone seeking to
strengthen their approach to getting and keeping
customers.
> —Charles I. Plosser, Dean
> William E. Simon Graduate School
> of Business Administration

> Paul Goldner uses illustrations from the current
> business world to provide concrete steps to make
> a difference in our business.
>> —Richard Diener
>> National Sales Manager
>> CreaNova, Inc.

The message has been increasingly clear through the end of the 1990s that success in sales now demands a far more strategic approach to customer development than ever before. Everyone knows that fact. What few know is HOW. In *Red-Hot Customers*, Paul Goldner lays out a practical blueprint that can be followed by any salesperson—selling in any market—to actually implement this new success strategy. And he does it better than anyone else.

—Art Siegel, Publisher
SalesDoctors Magazine

The nature of sales is undergoing a dramatic facelift. As the last bastion of corporate change, today's salesperson must be willing to toss out many of the past principles over ways to become a success. For sure, there is no longer any guaranteed selling system that works for salesperson and buyer alike. Paul Goldner accurately guides the reader on a course that properly projects how selling must function in the coming decades.

—Michael Reagan, CPSP
President
National Association
of Sales Professionals

Red-Hot Customers
How to Get Them,
How to Keep Them

Paul S. Goldner

Chandler House Press
Worcester, Massachusetts
1999

Red-Hot Customers:
How to Get Them, How to Keep Them

Copyright © 1999 by Sales & Performance Group, LLC

ISBN 1-886284-39-3
Library of Congress Catalog Card Number 98-89746
First Edition
ABCDEFGHIJK

Published by
Chandler House Press
335 Chandler Street
Worcester, MA 01602 USA

President
Lawrence J. Abramoff

Publisher/Editor-in-Chief
Richard J. Staron

Editorial/Production Manager
Jennifer J. Goguen

Director of Retail Sales and Marketing
Claire Cousineau Smith

Book Design and Production
CWL Publishing Enterprises
3010 Irvington Way
Madison, WI 53713 USA
www.execpc.com/cwlpubent

Chandler House Press books are available at special discounts for bulk purchases. For more information about how to arrange such purchases, please contact Chandler House Press, 335 Chandler Street, Worcester, MA 01602, or call (800) 642-6657, or fax (508) 756-9425, or find us on the World Wide Web at www.tatnuck.com.

Chandler House Press books are distributed to the trade by
National Book Network
4720 Boston Way
Lanham, MD 20706
(800) 462-6420

**To
Susan,
Jacqueline, and
Elissa**

**who continue to add
great value to my life!**

Contents

Acknowledgments

To Dick Staron and his team
at Chandler House Press,
and
To Paula Soto, my team at
the Sales and Performance Group,

Who all helped to make this project a Red-Hot success!

Introduction

Red-Hot Sales

Have you ever really wanted to buy something in your life? Of course you have. We all have. What happens when you really, really want to buy something?

If you're like me, there's a little voice that speaks to you from inside your head. The voice keeps telling you to buy. In fact, the voice keeps telling you to buy, no matter what!

Sometimes you cannot afford the item, but the voice keeps talking. Your mind and heart are saying yes, even though your wallet or budget is saying no.

We all know the end result. The end result is, of course, a sale. In fact, the end result is what I like to call a *red-hot* sale!

There are various motivating factors that can place you in this red-hot state. It could be because of advertising, something that you saw on the television or heard on the radio. It could be because of a friend who also purchased the same item. And, your red-hot sale could be because of prior positive experiences with a company or sales person.

If you are reading this book, in all likelihood you are a sales professional, a businessperson, or an entrepreneur. If you fall into any of these categories, sales—or should I say *successful* sales—are crucial to your success.

This book is designed to make your sales career red-hot.

We are going to do this through two means.

First, we are going to show you how to deliver your message to the market in a manner that will drive your prospects and customers crazy!

Second, we are going to show you how to make your customers so successful that they will beat a path to your door!

When you think about it, your sales world really consists of two parts.

First, there are those companies or individuals that have never done business with you. These are your *prospects*. How are you going to get your prospects to take the first step and buy from you?

Second, there are those companies or individuals that have already purchased from you. These are your *customers*. How are you going to keep them buying from you? And, how are you going to motivate them to buy more from you year in and year out?

These are your sales challenges.

I think the answer to these key questions lies in one word—excitement!

My feeling is that if you can get your prospects excited about what you do, they will take the first step and make, at least, a small purchase from you.

I also believe if you can get your customers excited about what you do, they will continue to buy more and more from you each year.

So, how do you breed excitement in sales?

The answer can, again, be summed up in one word—success!

Take a moment to reflect on your greatest achievements in life. I'm sure you were excited about your accomplishments. What caused your excitement?

Take a look at your greatest sales. I'm certain that both you and the customer were very excited about the transaction. What caused your excitement here?

My feeling is that success breeds excitement.

Be successful and you will be excited about your life. Make your customers successful and they will be excited about doing business with you. Make your prospects feel that they will be successful and they will be more likely to take the first step and buy from you.

Success breeds excitement.

This book is dedicated to breeding success in your sales career, and this book is dedicated to breeding success for your customers. The days of taking someone to lunch in order to develop a relationship are over. The good ol' boy and gal network for making sales is dead!

This is not to imply there is no place for good, old-fashioned relationship building in sales. There is. Building relationships by going out to lunch or playing a round of golf is great if you are first making your customer successful in business. Then, you can use the lunch or a round of golf to enhance your relationship.

But I do not believe that you can use golf or lunch to build your relationship in the absence of business performance. You must perform in order to be successful in sales. Only after you have made me successful does a lunch, a round of golf, or a ball game add to the relationship.

Let me illustrate.

Assume that I was a stockbroker and had a great investment opportunity. Suppose that I was able to convince you to invest $1,000 in my plan. Imagine that the investment grew and grew very rapidly. In fact, after one week, I had doubled your investment. After two weeks, your investment had doubled again, and after four weeks, your investment had doubled for a third time.

What type of relationship would we have?

I think our relationship would be great! It would be great even though I had never taken you to lunch. Success breeds excitement and I made you quite successful. In this simple circumstance, I would say our relationship was red-hot. In fact, if I called you up after our four-week relationship and presented a second $1,000 investment opportunity, my feeling is that you would buy.

Now let's take a look at the opposite circumstance.

Again, you invested $1,000 in my plan. However, this time the results were the opposite. Instead of your investment doubling after the first week, it diminished by 50%. In fact, the investment diminished by another 50% after the next week and a 50% again after the next two weeks. At this point, we are four weeks into our relationship and you are left with only $125 of your $1,000 investment.

How would our relationship be at this point? And how about if I took you to a ball game?

You see, success breeds excitement. In order to make your customers red-hot, and in order to make your sales career red-hot, you have to make your customers successful.

And just how do you make your customers successful? How do you raise them to that red-hot level of excitement where they cannot get enough of your product or service? How do you raise them to that level of excitement where they tell all of their friends and help you build your business through red-hot referrals and references?

Well, that's why I wrote this book. I have used the tools in this book to build my first business from zero dollars in sales to almost $100 million dollars in sales in just 12 years. I have used the tools in this book to launch and succeed at my second career, that of a professional speaker and sales trainer. I will use the tools in this book to develop my third career, that of a boxing promoter, and I will also use the tools in this book to build my fourth career, that of a restaurateur.

The tools, strategies, and ideas in this book work.

And these tools, strategies, and ideas will work in your business.

As you will see, businesses are built on filling needs. And where there is a customer with a need, there is the opportunity for success and excitement.

I can remember recently working with one of my customers, an Indian diamond merchant, at a trade show. I was there to observe how he used the ideas I had presented in a recent seminar. My favorite part of the presentation came when he cradled a piece of jewelry in his hands. His eyes began to twinkle as he presented the piece to the customer.

Where there is a customer with a need, you too have the opportunity to cradle your product, service, or idea in your hands as you present it to the customer. There is nothing more beautiful on the face of the earth than a product, service, or idea that fills the unique needs of your customers and prospects.

Part of the success of all red-hot sellers is that they have the ability to see the diamonds that lie within their products. They have the ability to understand the needs of their customers and prospects. More important, they have the ability to develop unique solutions for the needs of their customers. It is these solutions that form the basis of the red-hot sales process.

However, just because we see the diamonds that lie within our products and services does not mean the customers and prospects will see the same thing. Helping your customers and prospects see what you see and understand what you understand is why I wrote this book.

Your success will come from the strategies and ideas contained in this book as well as a lot of persistence and hard work on your part. It is for this reason that I have developed "The Three Traits of All Red-Hot Sales Professionals."

These traits will serve as your beacon of light and your guiding force in the field. Throughout this book, we will return to these three principles time and time again for the answers to our challenges.

If we believe in these principles, they will guide us to success. If we do not believe in these principles, our sales careers and our sales results will be as unpredictable as the movements of a ship without a rudder. We will have no way to stay on course.

The Three Traits of All Red-Hot Sales Professionals

I first learned about the three traits of all red-hot sales professionals when I started my first business in 1983. I left a successful career with the public accounting firm of Price Waterhouse and started a computer training company.

When I left Price Waterhouse, friends, relatives, and colleagues asked me why I was giving up a promising career in public accounting for the perils of owning my own business.

At the time, I believed that all I had to do to be successful was open up my own business. I thought my success would be automatic.

I later came across a great story that summed up my thoughts at the start of my entrepreneurial and sales career. It was a story about John Paul Getty, the oil executive and billionaire. Getty was being interviewed about his formula for success.

When the interviewer asked Getty how he accounted for his great success, Getty replied, "Some people discover oil, and others don't."

When I started my first business, I felt that I would discover oil.

I had one partner at the time and we started our business on $3,000 in working capital. We rented space in a small office in New York City. Our beginnings were so humble that we didn't have enough money to buy two desks, two chairs, and two telephones so that we could both sit at one time.

However, we were sure that we would discover oil. We were sure that our success was just around the corner.

Much to our surprise, our success was not automatic and our $3,000 war chest was soon running low. Fortunately, we were able to change our ways and grow our business into one with offices throughout the United States and Canada and almost $100,000,000 in sales.

As I look back on my career and particularly the growth of my first business, I believe that my success, and all selling success, can be traced back to three principles—"the three traits of all red-hot sales professionals."

I use these principles to guide me through my day-to-day selling activities. I present them here so that you too will have a guiding light for your sales career. I believe that I can overcome every sales challenge I face by referring back to these principles. If you put them into action and consistently rely on them for guidance and counsel, I believe they will be of similar value in your sales career.

Be Proactive in Creating Your Success

The first lesson I learned in growing my own business is that great sales people are proactive in the creation of their own success. Being proactive in the creation of your own success means that you take ultimate responsibility for your sales results.

In sales, you can divide everything into two categories: those things that you can change and those things that you can't.

Those things that you can't change include changes in the economic climate, changes in the political climate, mergers, divestitures, and other sales-related factors that are simply beyond your control.

As I work with companies around the globe in improving sales organization effectiveness, I find this one point alone to be one of the greatest impediments to selling success. Many sales people spend much of their time focusing on areas where they cannot have an impact.

It shouldn't take a great deal of thought to understand that working in an area where you cannot have an impact will do little to advance your sales career.

Great sales people, on the other hand, always focus their efforts on areas where they can have an impact. Great sales people do not worry about the economic climate, for example. They will be successful in any economic environment. Great sales people do not worry about the political climate. They will be successful under any political condition.

Great sales people take the good and the bad in their sales career and then they start to develop their next step. In fact, this is what makes sales such a great profession! There is always—and I want to emphasize the word *always*—a next step. There is always something that you can be doing to better your chances of success in the sales cycle.

Great sales people focus on where they can have an impact, not where they cannot.

My favorite example of being proactive in the creation of one's own success can be found in a postcard I recently received. The card was from a local real estate brokerage company and it read as follows. (Please note that some of the names have been changed to protect the innocent.)

Dear Mr. And Mrs. Goldner:

Diane Jones and I congratulate you on the second anniversary in your home on Tree-Lined Lane.

We hope that the past two years were wonderful, and that the coming year will be filled with happiness!

Sincerely,

Pat Dixon
Manager
Anywhere Office

I'm sure that you have your own stationery for short, handwritten notes like this to customers and prospects.

And I'm sure that you are writing letters like this to your customers and prospects to enhance your chances of making sales. All great sales people do!

What makes this letter so special is that the person who wrote the letter was not the person we purchased our home from. In fact, we've never even met this person!

I believe that great sales people are proactive in the creation of their own success and this is one great example of a proactive sales person. The simple effort of sending me this letter illustrates three key selling points.

First, the agent understands that sales are a *process*, not an *event*. She is simply starting the process with my wife and I.

As you will see in reading this book, my approach to sales is to first find the very best prospects and customers in the marketplace and then place them into a business development process.

The role of the business development process is to educate your prospects and customers about the value you bring to the relationship. If customers and prospects understand the value we bring to market, they will be more likely to buy from us—and to continue to buy from us.

This sales person also understands the value in being first to customer, a point we are going to discuss extensively in this book. Many sales people prefer to be last to customer. Being last to customer means that the customer has received all competing bids and you now have to the opportunity to meet or beat the lowest competing bid to win the sale.

I do not believe that you can be successful in sales competing on price. If you compete on price, you may eventually reach the point where the price of your product or service is zero.

Rather, I believe that you must compete on value, and I believe that the earlier you enter the sales cycle, the greater your opportunity to establish the value of your offer.

Finally, this sales person understands that after a sale takes place, a new sales cycle starts. Obviously, she is starting to move into position for success in my next sales cycle or home-buying experience.

In fact, I am so impressed with this agent's proactivity that I have kept her business card and will call her should the need arise to buy a new home in the area. Should the need not arise for me, I still can refer this person to friends and relatives, should they need to purchase a home.

Before we move on to the next trait of all red-hot sales professionals, I would like to make one additional point. You could be reading this book and be skeptical about the last story. After all, the sales person who wrote that note may be about 28 years away from her next potential sale with me.

As you go through your sales career, you never want to ask, "Do the ideas I read in this book really work?" As you go through your sales career, you never want to ask, "Do the ideas I learn about in the seminars I attend really work?" Finally, as you go through your sales career, you never want to ask, "Do the ideas that my boss or co-workers share with me really work?" The question you never want to ask in sales is "Do these ideas work?" The real question to ask yourself in sales is "What happens if I don't?"

The point I am making is, if you send a letter to a prospect like the one I received, do you really know if the letter will enhance your chances of being successful in the sales cycle? Of course you don't. Neither do I.

However, what you do know is that if you do not send the letter, you will clearly not progress in the sales cycle. The only guarantee in sales is this: if you do nothing, you get nothing. I always say, "Even a lottery winner must first buy a ticket."

If you are proactive in the creation of your success, you always have at least a puncher's chance. (For those of you who are not boxing fans, a puncher's chance is that one lucky punch that turns a fight around for a boxer, from a defeat into a victory.) In other words, if you continue to try, you never know what can happen.

To me, failure in selling is not in winning or losing a sale. Failure in selling is not in achieving or not achieving your sales goals. Rather, failure in selling is in being in the same position two years in a row. There is simply no excuse for that. And that is why I love sales. I love sales because there is always something that you can be doing to enhance your chances of success in the sales cycle. Red-hot sales professionals are always proactive in the creation of their own success.

Think Strategically

The second lesson I learned in building my business is that to succeed in sales, you must be a strategic thinker. A strategic thinker understands that most sales take place after the fifth call—and that most sales people quit after the first.

A strategic thinker understands that you cannot be successful in sales if you do not bring new and valuable information to your customer at each point of contact in the sales cycle.

A strategic thinker knows that if one idea does not work with a particular account, there are a number—in fact an infinite number—

of other ways that you can approach the customer or prospect the next time through the sales cycle.

Recently, I read an article about a sales professional who had lost a major account that was generating about $250,000 in annual business volume. He was obviously upset over the loss and tried very hard to regain the business. However, his efforts were without success. His problem? He was not thinking strategically.

If you had read the story carefully, you would have learned that the sales person was trying to penetrate the account using old ideas. He went back to the same people he had always worked with and presented them with the same ideas. He saw no reason to change his approach and the customer saw no reason to change their decision.

In sales, as in all of life, if you do the same things, you can expect the same results. Strategic thinkers understand when a plan is not working and they develop another.

When our sales person realized his initial plan would bear no fruit, he began to look for other ways to penetrate the account. He started working with a person with whom he had never worked before, a manager assigned with the task of moving the company into a new market.

The company had no experience in the new market and the sales person saw the manager struggling over his decisions. When the sales person began to question the new manager, he learned that the new market was one in which the sales person had worked on a prior job.

The sales person saw no opportunity for an immediate sale, but he forged ahead and was able to help the manager with some of his decisions. As the sales person put it, he noted how the company began to perceive him differently as a result of the process. The company continued to request information from him and, eventually, the company started to buy again. In fact, the sales person was not only able to regain the account, but even grew it. What had been a $250,000-per-year account was now generating in excess of $1,000,000 in sales. The key to success, in this instance, was strategic thinking.

The lesson in this story is that there are always a number of ways to approach an account. If you think strategically, you will use your creative imagination to develop new approaches to developing your customer relationships. If you think in a linear manner, you will see only one way to approach and develop a relationship. All red-hot sales professionals think strategically.

Focus on Your Customers

The final key to your success in red-hot sales is perhaps your most important. In order to make your sales career red-hot, you must make your customers red-hot. The only way to make your customers red-hot is through extreme customer focus.

There is a book by Dr. Norman Vincent Peale, the author of *The Power of Positive Thinking*, that best defines extreme customer focus.

The book is called *Stay Alive All of Your Life* and relates the story of a small-town furniture storeowner. His business was not doing well. In fact, the store was on the verge of bankruptcy. As you might expect, the storeowner was quite distraught and went to Peale for consolation and advice. The storeowner told Peale about a particular source of frustration—a woman who would come by his store every day to look at a chair in his window. He could not understand why the woman would not come into his store to buy. That one passerby exasperated the storeowner. Here's what Peale had to say:

> Think first of helping Mrs. X. And to do that you must first get to know her and her family; study her needs.

What Peale is telling us is that the key to successful selling is to first understand your customers' needs. This is one of the foundation points of the red-hot sales process. I believe that you can make a sale even without customer needs. However, I do not believe that without customer needs you can build a relationship.

One of the keys to successful selling is building long-term relationships with your customers. The starting point of the relationship-building process is a need on the part of the customer.

Peale continues by noting:

> Do not think so much about putting her money in your pocket as putting your chair, which she needs, into her home. Do this with all of your customers. Think of them as people needing your goods instead of yourself needing their money.

There are two key learning points here.

First, customers need us as much as we need them. If your company were to lose all of its customers, it is quite clear that the company would not be successful.

However, the converse of this statement is also true. Where would your company be without quality providers of products and services? My feeling is it would be in exactly the same place. A company cannot exist without customers and a company cannot exist without quality providers of products and services. As long as you add value in the sales cycle, your customers need you as much as you need them.

The additional point made by Peale is that this woman is not an exception. All of the storeowner's customers—actual and potential—are in the exact same position. They all have needs and he is in a position to provide solutions to those needs.

Peale then concludes his comments by giving us what I would consider to be the red-hot sales professional's mission statement:

Find ways of helping them overcome their difficulties, and you will overcome your own in so doing.

Plainly stated, Peale tells us to learn about our customers, study their needs, and solve their problems. If we do this successfully, we will, in turn, be successful. We will, in turn, be red-hot!

Where Do We Go from Here?

Proactivity, strategy, and customer focus. These are the core skills of all red-hot sales professionals. These are also the principles and values that underlie this book—"how to make your customers red-hot and how to make your sales career red-hot."

The remainder of this book will give you your redprint, I mean blueprint, for success.

The book is divided into two parts.

First, we will talk about how to take your message to market. Remember that your target market is made up of both prospects and customers.

Your challenge with *prospects* is how to get them to take the first step and buy from you.

I think this challenge is formidable.

I believe that the single biggest impediment to a sale is the customer asking, "Am I making the right choice?" The easiest way to overcome this obstacle is with a proven track record of success with the customer.

However, we are talking about your *prospects* here.

How do you overcome this obstacle without the benefit of a proven track record? That's the focus of the first section of the book: how to take your message to market, how to make your prospects so red-hot they will be willing to take the first step with you even though you do not have a proven track record with them.

Your challenge with *customers* is clear. Keep them coming back for more and more.

The second section of the book is designed to show you how to penetrate your key accounts and how to build barriers to keep out the competition. After all, once you succeed with an account, your best accounts will be another's best prospects. How do you defend the turf you worked so hard to win?

Let's get started by taking our message to market and developing our red-hot cause. That's the first chapter of this book.

Chapter 1

Defining Your Red-Hot Cause

Have you ever wondered what separates the top-performing companies from the rest of the pack? How could Microsoft excel like it has? Why would Intel dominate the market? What made Wal-Mart so special?

Have you ever wondered what separates great sales people from the others? Why do top performers excel month in and month out while others never seem to break out of mediocrity?

Like newborn babies, all companies start out equal. Great companies are made; they do not spawn from incorporation papers filed in a lawyer's office. Just as great companies are made, great sales people are also made. (Just check your birth certificate if you are unsure.)

I have always wondered what separates top performers, either corporations or individuals, from the rest of the pack. As I delivered my seminars around the world, I began to study this very question. Here's what I found!

I was delivering a program and selected an individual from the audience. I asked him if he tries hard when he goes to work. I'm sure you can guess what he said. Of course he tries hard!

I then went to another individual in the audience. I asked her if she gives it 110% when she goes to work. Just as you would have answered, she responded with an emphatic yes!

I went to a third individual in the group and I asked him if, when he sees an opportunity for the company, he takes advantage of the opportunity so that the company may benefit. Of course!

Finally, I opened the discussion to the rest of the audience. I asked if they would have answered my questions any differently from my three individuals. They all agreed that they would have responded in exactly the same manner.

I was surprised to see such a dedicated group of individuals, but figured that I was working with a very special company. I concluded the program and went on to my next assignment, where I asked the very same questions.

I was working with a different company, but the responses were identical. I was surprised again, so I repeated this process over and over. I asked the same questions in the United States, Canada, Switzerland, and India. The responses never varied.

I was confused.

If the world is full of such dedicated employees, why are some companies performing at a higher level than others? If those people are all doing their very best, why are some individuals performing at a higher level than others?

The answer, I learned, is that some companies and some individuals have a great cause, a red-hot cause, something they would pursue until their last breath. Lesser-performing companies and lesser-performing individuals simply lack purpose. They lack direction. They lack a great cause.

It is the great cause, the red-hot cause, that separates leaders from the rest of the pack.

If you study your history books, business or otherwise, you will see that history is full of great causes.

Take a look at World War II, for example. Were the soldiers who fought in the war there for the great salary and benefits? Of course not. They were there to support a great cause.

Take a look at Chrysler Corporation when it faced bankruptcy during the early 1970s. What was the driving force behind its turn-around? Some would argue that it was the federal subsidies. I would argue that it was pride. After all, Chrysler was one of the Big Three, an American institution. The employees of Chrysler couldn't just let it perish.

How about the Chicago Bulls of the 1990s? What was their driving force? Some would argue that it was Michael Jordan. I would argue that, while Jordan was certainly a great contributor, an even greater factor was the cause. After all, their first goal was to win an NBA championship (the cause). Their second goal was to repeat (the cause) and their third goal was to threepeat (the cause). After Jordan returned to the NBA from a brief stint as a professional baseball player, there was a new driving force, this time to regain the championship (the cause) and then to repeat again (the cause).

You see, behind any great achievement, there is a driving cause, a red-hot cause, something that drives an individual or a corporation to superior performance.

A driving force can also motivate individuals. What caused President John F. Kennedy or Martin Luther King, Jr. to achieve their high levels of success and to ultimately sacrifice their lives? Again, it was a red-hot cause.

Why does a great cause impact your success?

I believe the answer to this question is both simple and profound.

Imagine you are in a room full of people and there's a ball in the middle of the room. Imagine a string tied from the ball to each person's waist. Finally, imagine that the instruction is given to pull the ball.

Where does the ball go?

The answer is clearly unpredictable. The ball could move in the direction of the most people or the strongest people, or it could stay in the same place and not move at all.

Unfortunately, this is how most businesses are run. Employees are given instructions to work hard, but the instructions lack a specific direction. The results, in this case as with the ball, will be quite unpredictable and the company will rarely succeed.

In the same manner, most individuals also lack direction. They go to work every single day and they try hard, but they do not have a goal in mind. Remember what Lily Tomlin said: "I always wanted to be someone when I grew up. I guess I should have been a little more specific."

In order to be successful, you must have a goal. You must have a target. You must have a motivating force. This is particularly true in sales, because the world of sales is filled with obstacles and rejection. How are you going to overcome the obstacles, how are you going to overcome the rejection, if you don't have a driving force, a red-hot cause that gives you purpose day in and day out?

Let's go back to our example of the ball for a moment. A look at the alternative provides some interesting insights.

Imagine that everyone in the room is given some direction and asked to pull the ball toward the front of the room. Where does the ball go now?

Not only does the ball go to the front of the room, it moves in that direction very rapidly. You see, when a company has a red-hot cause, everyone pulls the ball in the same direction and the company excels. Just as companies can benefit from focus and a red-hot cause, so can individual sales people.

My experience with sales and sales people (myself included) is that most sales people tend to follow the path of least resistance. What is the path of least resistance? This is the path that will entail the least amount of rejection.

The least amount of rejection in a sales environment typically means that you will work only with your best customers. The result: no rejection, but no growth either. The least amount of rejection also means that you will gravitate to the smaller business opportunities in the market. (After all, the larger opportunities are the ones that everyone else is going after.)

In order to be successful in sales, you must have focus and you must have direction. You must have a red-hot cause.

How Can I Create My Red-Hot Cause?

There are actually three steps in defining your red-hot cause.

The first step is to decide which customers and prospects you wish to work with in the marketplace. We will show you how to do this in this chapter.

Once you have defined your target market, you must tell the market what it is that you stand for. You must begin to answer the toughest question in all of sales—"Why should I do business with you?" Again, we will begin this discussion here.

Finally, after you have defined your target market and after you have answered the question, "Why should I do business with you?", you must package your market position in a manner that will maximize your sales results. This topic will be the focus of Chapter 2.

How to Define Your Target Market

Having started and grown two successful businesses, I can assure you that focus is one of the fundamental tenets of business success. When I started my first business in 1983, we had $3,000 in working capital and no customers. I was so desperate for a sale that I believe I would have done anything (legal and ethical) to generate some revenue. However, just selling anything to anybody does not create a world-class computer training company. Rather, selling computer training to world-class organizations creates a world-class computer training company.

We didn't know this at the time and so our first approach to sales and marketing was to assume that everyone could use computer training. If you think back to 1983, and even if you consider the technology environment today, the assumption that everyone could use computer training may very well be a good one. We believed this at the time and built our sales and marketing strategy around this one premise.

What we learned was that, although everyone may very well need computer training, there was a much better approach to sales. What we learned was that everything in sales is governed by one simple rule.

The overriding truth in professional sales is that there are only 24 hours in the day. You cannot change this. This means that the time you can invest in the sales process is clearly fixed, at some point below 24 hours. Your goal, in sales, becomes to sell as much as you can in the fixed time you have to invest in the sales process.

The only way you can do this is to decide who are your very best prospects.

Before we get into a discussion of how to define "best" as it relates to your customers and prospects, one additional point of clarification is required.

How to Be a Top-Performing Account Manager

If you were to study account managers and place them into cate-gories on the basis of sales performance, what you would find is that account managers or sales professionals can be placed into three categories.

First, there are *new* account managers. A new account manager is one who is new to a business and, as a result, is producing very little in the way of current revenue.

The second category of account manager is what I call *moderate*. A moderate account manager is one who has been in the business for a while and is producing a moderate level of business volume. A moderate account manager might be in the fiftieth percentile of the standard bell curve. There are plenty of account managers who are doing better, but there are also plenty of account managers who are doing worse.

The third category of account manager is the one that we all aspire to. It is the *top* account manager. Top account managers are those who are producing sales among the very best in their business.

If you were to take a look at the collection of sales for the three major categories of sales professional, they might appear as pre-sented in Figure 1-1.

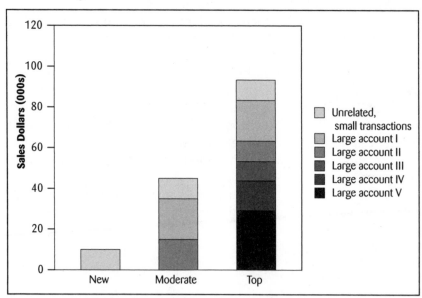

Figure 1-1. Sales development chart

The sales of those in the *new* category would tend to be composed of a relatively larger number of smaller accounts. The types of relationships would tend to be more transactional in nature and the sales volume in any given account would tend to be small.

The sales of those in the *moderate* category would contain a small number of large accounts and a larger number of small accounts. In fact, you can see that the difference between the *new* and *moderate* categories is those few large accounts.

It is important, at this point, to understand what I mean by a "large" account. To me, a large account is not one where you happen to make one large sale. Rather, a large account is one where you can consistently count on a steady and heavy volume of sales throughout the year.

For example, a large account might provide you with $10,000 of business per month. This is in contrast to an account where you receive a one-time sale of $100,000. I would not consider the second account a large account in spite of the volume of the sale. In order to turn the second account into a large account, you would have to further develop the account so that the level of sales would be both large and consistent.

Referring back to Figure 1-1, you can see that if you are a *new* account manager you must review your collection of accounts and start to determine or develop a strategy to obtain your first large account. Once you obtain your first large account, you need to think about getting your second large account and then your third. By the time you have several large accounts, you will have sufficient volume to move into the moderate category.

If you are an account manager in the *moderate* category, you should focus your efforts on building your base of large accounts. What separates the *moderate* and the *top* categories of account managers is simply the number of accounts that are in their respective bases.

Your base is that subset of your sales that is made up of only your large accounts. It is typically the magnitude of your base that determines your success over the long run in sales.

If you return to Figure 1-1, you can see that a sales person in the *new* category has no base. This means that he or she must start from zero sales each month and work very hard to develop a current book of business. That person's sales consist largely of a series of unrelated transactions.

However, if you look at the portfolio of a *moderate* sales person, what you should notice is that he or she has both a base, a set of sales to count on month in and month out, and a series of transactions on top of the base. It is the base, however, that accounts for this person's better performance.

Finally, if you look at the sales of the *top* producers, you notice an extensive base and also a series of transactions on top of the base. Again, the base is what accounts for the consistently superior performance. The magnitude of the transactions on top of the base makes certain months more extraordinary than others for the top producers.

As you can see, what separates top performers from the rest of the pack is simply following a large-account strategy. The question now becomes "How do you implement a large-account strategy in your business?"

How to Implement a Large-Account Strategy

In order to implement a large-account strategy, you must consider two factors. First, you must consider the sales volume of your existing customers. Second, and perhaps more important, you must consider future potential, not only of accounts that you are doing business with, but also of accounts that you should be doing business with.

The easy part of the process is starting with accounts that you are currently doing business with.

Imagine that you are selling computers and your largest accounts are those with which you are doing in excess of $100,000 per year. These would be your "A" accounts.

Assume that your "B" accounts, your moderate-sized accounts, are those customers that generate between $50,000 and $99,999 in annual business volume.

Your "C" accounts would then be those accounts that are generating less than $50,000 per year.

Figure 1-2 shows you how to rank your existing customers based on business volume.

However, in order to be successful in sales, you must do more than just rank your customers in terms of *current* business volume.

	Business Volume
A	$100,000 or more
B	$50,000-$99,999
C	$1-$49,999

Figure 1-2. Account classification based on business volume

You must also look at prospects based on *future* business potential.

As I mentioned earlier, most sales people follow the path of least resistance. The path of least resistance in sales is where you will minimize your level of rejection.

You can minimize your level of rejection by working with your best customers. Your best customers will clearly be most receptive to your sales message, since they are already purchasing a large amount of your product or service. However, if you never look beyond your best customers, you may be missing some exciting opportunities and limiting your future growth potential.

You can also minimize your chances of rejection by working with the smaller accounts in the marketplace. Most sales people assume that these accounts will be easier to penetrate than the larger business opportunities. Unfortunately, this strategy may also limit your future growth potential.

In order to be successful in sales, you must consider future growth potential when you define your target market. By considering future growth potential, you will be certain to develop a strategy that will maximize your return on investment.

To consider future growth potential, you must look at the customers and prospects in your market and decide on a measurement or statistic to estimate future buying potential.

There are several key points here.

First, in any business, there is always some measurement that can be used to estimate future buying potential. More often than not, this measurement can be the size of the company as determined by either its gross sales or the number of employees in the company.

For example, my business is sales training. A good measure of buying potential for my customers is simply their gross sales. The more sales they have, the more likely they are to need sales training.

I could also use employee count as a measure of buying potential for my customers. Again, the more employees, the more likely the customer is to need my services.

In effect, we are saying that larger companies have greater buying potential than smaller companies. This should make sense in most businesses.

If sales or employee count do not work in your business, select another measurement. Other measurements that have worked well are the number of locations a company has or the size of its facilities. We are simply trying to separate the accounts with larger potential from the smaller ones.

Let's go back to our example of selling computers. Assuming that we select the number of employees as the way to measure future buying potential, Figure 1-3 shows us how we might segment our market on the basis of future buying potential.

	Employee Count
A	5,000 or more
B	1,000-4,999
C	500-999

Figure 1-3. Account classification based on future buying potential

The point I am trying to make is that you want to work with prospects that are very likely to become large accounts. The key here is to define a process through which you can identify the accounts that are more likely to be large.

I have often heard sales people say that an account *feels* like a good account. My question is "What does a good account feel like?" Is it soft or is it hard? Is it round or is it square? I think you get the point. Finding the good accounts should not be a random event, based on feelings. Rather, it should be the result of a well-defined process.

The second point to understand in this process is that the factor you select to measure buying potential needs only be an estimate. It does not have to be a 100% accurate predictor of the future.

If we look at the size of a company, as measured by gross sales, what we are trying to estimate is that the larger companies will, on average, be larger accounts and that the smaller companies, on average, will be smaller accounts.

This does not guarantee that IBM, for example, will be a large account. Our approach only suggests that the IBMs of the world are more likely to be larger accounts.

Conversely, our method does not rule out Paul's Widget Company (a smaller company in the market) from being a large account. Rather, it suggests that companies like Paul's Widget Company will tend to be smaller accounts in your sales portfolio.

The third key point in this process is that we have chosen not to work with certain accounts in the market. If you refer back to Figure 1-3, you will notice our "C" category accounts are those with 500 to 999 employees. The reason we did this is to fine-tune our market focus.

Many sales professionals take what I call the "all" approach to market focus. The "all" approach to market focus suggests that any customer is a good customer.

Although I would never turn down an order, I think it's important to take a close look at the logic behind the "all" approach.

In sales, there are better customers and there are worse customers. Also, in most businesses, one sales person will not have the time to work with every customer and prospect in the market.

Because you will not have the opportunity to work with every possible customer and prospect in the market, you have to make a decision as to which ones you want to work with.

Do you want to work with the *better* customers or the *worse* customers?

This is clearly a rhetorical question.

The answer, of course, is that you want to work with the better customers. The better customers in our case are the customers with the larger future buying potential.

In our example, we set a lower boundary of 500 employees. This means that if a company has 501 employees, it is in our target market and we will proactively work with it.

However, if the company does not have 500 employees (whether it has 4 or 499 employees), it is outside our target market and we will leave it to a different method of cultivation. (We'll discuss these different methods shortly.)

We set the lower boundary of 500 employees to yield a manageable number of accounts for the account manager or company. If the number of accounts that results from setting a lower limit of 500 is still too high, you can always raise the lower limit and focus your efforts even more.

If, on the other hand, you find that you have worked with every company in your target market and still have plenty of time, you can always be less discriminating and lower the limit to let more accounts into the fold.

In the beginning you want to be more focused. When you set your lower boundary, be more discriminating and err on the high side. You can always lower the limit later and take on new accounts and prospects.

There is one final piece of advice that I would like to offer. You may be in what I would call a mature market. A mature market is one in which all of the customers and prospects are known and you have the time to work with most, if not all, of them. The commodity chemical business might be a good example of this type of business.

If you are in a mature market, you will still benefit from this type of future potential analysis. You may not eliminate accounts on the basis of future buying potential, simply because there are not enough accounts in the market. However, you will benefit by having a strong market focus and by understanding the investment you should be making with each account in the market.

We have now looked at our accounts both on the basis of historical performance and on the basis of future buying potential. Which method is better?

The answer is neither. Rather, you may want to consider using both to get your best results.

Figure 1-4 presents our approach of segmenting your market on the basis of current business volume and future buying potential. This system segments your target market into nine categories, A1 through C3. The purpose of this system is to help you maximize the return you receive on the time you invest in the sales cycle.

Your A1, A2, and A3 accounts would be your *top-priority* accounts.

	A = 5,000+	B = 1,000-4,999	C = 500-999
1=$100,000+	A1	B1	C1
2=$50,000-$99,999	A2	B2	C2
3=$1-$49,999	A3	B3	C3

Figure 1-4. Account classification based on both current volume and future buying potential

These are the accounts that I would call and visit most frequently.

Why? These accounts are going to produce the greatest results over the long run.

The B1 and C1 accounts are what I would call my *maintenance* accounts. These accounts contribute significantly to current volume but have less growth potential than my top-priority accounts.

While I would never ignore these accounts, I would make only the investments necessary to ensure continued business volume at current levels.

Finally, your B2, B3, C2, and C3 accounts are what I would consider *lower-priority* accounts. These are the accounts that I would work with only after I have fully covered my high-priority and maintenance accounts. They represent both smaller current business volume and limited future growth potential.

Please note that, although your lower-priority accounts are not as good as your high-priority accounts or your maintenance accounts, they are still good accounts! Remember that we limited our target market to companies with 500 or more employees. This means there are a number of companies in the market that we are not contacting because they have fewer than 500 employees. In other words, any company within your target market has the potential to be a good customer. It is the companies outside our target market that we need to be careful about spending our time with.

The purpose of defining your target market is to make certain that you are always moving toward your business objectives. We all know that sales is a business fraught with rejection and even the most hardened of us prefer to avoid rejection. In sales this avoidance takes the form of following the path of least resistance. The path of least resistance often leads to working with companies outside your target market.

ɜ your target market will help you keep your eye on the
make certain that you are following the straightest path
r business objectives.

I would like to make one final comment about defining your target market. This process is a great starting point for your selling success. However, as you get to know your customers better, use the
knowledge you obtain to upgrade the quality of your account classi-
fications. What might appear like an A1 account on paper might not
turn out to be an A1 account after several face-to-face customer vis-
its. This is a dynamic system and should always be upgraded on the
basis of your knowledge of the customer.

How Should I Handle Accounts Outside My Target Market?

I always get asked the question, "How should I handle accounts outside my target market?" The approach to accounts outside your target market is a function of the resources you have to invest in culti-
vating the market.

If you have limited resources, I would suggest investing your
resources where you will get the greatest impact. This is clearly
within your target market.

If you have extensive resources, I would suggest covering your
market as described in Figure 1-5. This chart shows how you can
divide the accounts outside your target market into three additional
categories: better accounts, moderate accounts, and smaller
accounts.

The process used to make these distinctions would be the same
as the one outlined above for accounts within your target market.

A1, A2, A3 Accounts	Top-priority accounts
B1, C1 Accounts	Maintenance accounts
B2, B3, C2, C3 Accounts	Lower-priority accounts
Better accounts outside your target market	Call center
Moderate accounts outside your target market	Distribution channels
Smaller accounts outside your target market	Direct mail

Figure 1-5. How to cover your entire market

Once you have categorized the accounts outside your target market, you need to invest in these other market segments commensurate with the returns they might generate.

My recommendation is to assign the larger accounts outside your target market to a call center. A call center is staffed with company employees who do not visit the customer. Rather, they handle most of their business on the telephone, a more cost-effective means of selling.

Accounts below your call center accounts should be assigned to an external distribution system. Finally, the smallest accounts in the market could be handled through a direct mail program. The prospects in this segment of the market would receive a live sales effort only when they are ready to place an order.

Your Value Proposition

Now that we have defined our target market, we must develop our *value proposition*. Your value proposition is designed to tell the market what you are uniquely qualified to deliver. Your value proposition is that combination of both product and service that you bring to market. It is your complete offering.

It is important to understand that your value proposition includes both the product or service sold by your company and all of the value-added items that you can put into the package. In fact, I would suggest that it is that layered value that really gives the customers what they are looking for, not the product or service itself. After all, which would you prefer, a state-of-the-art computer that you do not know how to operate or a less sophisticated model that comes with appropriate training and support? I would suggest that your return on investment would be greater with the latter option.

As you develop your value proposition, make certain that it is truly valued by the market. A value proposition that is not valued by customers and prospects will do little to promote your success. While this may seem like a trivial point, it warrants additional discussion.

In order to be valued by customers and prospects, the items you are bringing to market must have a tangible bottom-line impact on their business. Remember that it is *customer success* that will be the driving force behind our red-hot selling efforts. If we can make our customers successful, they will line up to buy from us. They will also tell all of their friends and business colleagues about us. Most important, they will view us as more than a peddler of commodity products and services.

I once worked with a company that manufactured large pieces of industrial equipment. Its equipment was priced at a 40% premium in the marketplace. What made that company's value proposition successful was that it included next-day parts and service in a business where it was traditional to provide next-week parts and service.

My customer knew that the most critical concern for its customers was to keep the factories running. In fact, the average cost of factory downtime for its customers was $20,000 per hour. If a machine broke down even only once per year, it could double and even triple the true cost of the machine. By delivering next-day parts and service, the company was able to save its customers millions of dollars per year in reduced downtime. Reduced downtime clearly has a tangible bottom-line impact. In fact, the impact was so great that the company was able to maintain its premium pricing and leadership position in the market.

In addition to producing a tangible bottom-line impact for your customer, your value proposition must provide something that the customer sorely needs. Federal Express gave us a great application of this concept when it presented us with the opportunity "to absolutely, positively deliver packages overnight." My customer did the same thing by providing its customers with next-day parts and service when the traditional industry standard was next-week parts and service.

Should *I* Create My Red-Hot Cause?

At first glance, you might argue that your value proposition, your guiding force, or your red-hot cause is the responsibility of upper management. And I might be inclined to agree. In the case of Federal Express, the initial direction clearly came from upper management. However, if you consider your complete product or service offering, the basic product plus the value-added services, you will see that the sales person can have a major impact here.

One of my favorite sales stories concerns a tissue sales person selling to large hotel chains like the Marriott and the Hyatt. His red-hot cause was to have a complete understanding of how his customers used his product, tissues, in their business, operating large hotels.

When visiting his customers, he would often ask if he could work with hotel personnel to better understand their tissue usage. His discoveries were quite significant.

First, he learned that hotel cleaning staff were under a strict mandate by management to make certain that a guest room never ran out of tissues. This was important to the hotel because most hotel guests would be unhappy if they ran out of tissues in the middle of the night.

Second, he learned that hotel cleaning staff responded to this mandate by using a finger to make certain there was an appropriate supply of tissues in the room. This was obviously an imprecise method of determining tissue levels, which resulted in the disposal of boxes of tissues that were still half full and three-quarters full.

Here's where the sales person had the opportunity to put his red-hot cause to work for both the success of the customer and his own success. He began to wonder how many half-full boxes of tissues that hotel chain's cleaning staffs were disposing of worldwide. If the hotel he was visiting was any indication, there was an opportunity to have a significant bottom-line impact for his customer.

Further, the sales person also began to wonder how low the tissues could go before the box could be tossed without significant waste. To get an answer to that question, he surveyed the rooms before they were cleaned and determined that the average guest uses approximately eight tissues per day. On the basis of that information, he presented his customers with the brilliant recommendation to color code the last 16 tissues in the box. This would provide a sufficient margin for error and also minimize tissue waste worldwide.

As you can see, when you bundle a product or service with the expertise and the initiative of the sales person, you can have a considerable impact on both the offering you are bringing to the market and your ability to create or impact your red-hot cause.

The crucial point to understand here is that a red-hot cause is vital to your success. Without the guiding light of some force bigger than your commission check, you will be unable to sustain superior performance over the long run.

A red-hot cause is designed to last you a lifetime.

How to Create Your Red-Hot Cause

Your red-hot cause should be the summary of your business existence. Earlier, we discussed the red-hot causes used by American troops during World War II (freedom), by Lee Iacocca and Chrysler during the early 1970s (pride), and by Michael Jordan and the Chicago Bulls in the 1990s (the threepeat). We also discussed Martin Luther King, Jr. and John F. Kennedy and their driving forces.

To succeed in sales, you must have a red-hot cause, something you are willing to go to battle for.

In creating your red-hot cause, please keep two factors in mind.

First, your red-hot cause must always be *customer-focused*. Remember: customers are interested in their business, not yours. The customers are interested in their success, not yours. Your red-hot cause must have a tangible bottom-line impact on your customers.

Second, we discussed the idea of giving the customers *something they need, but do not already have*. Giving the customers what they already have is clearly not a source of value to the customers.

By way of example, my red-hot cause follows:

The $_{Bottom\ Line}$ in Sales Performance.

My goal, my red-hot cause as a professional speaker and sales trainer, is to improve my customers' bottom-line performance by helping them both sell more and sell more at higher prices.

Conclusion

The focus of this chapter was to help you define your red-hot cause. Your red-hot cause gives you two crucial tools for your selling success. First, your red-hot cause identifies your very best customers and prospects. Second, your red-hot cause helps you craft your message or value proposition for the market.

The next chapter is going to talk about how to implement your red-hot cause in the field so that your customers and prospects will start to form a line outside your door to buy from you!

Chapter 2

Delivering Your Red-Hot Cause to the Market

When my first book, *Red-Hot Cold Call Selling, Prospecting Techniques That Pay Off!* (AMACOM, 1995), was released, it was selected by Executive Book Summaries as one of the best business books of 1995. I had visions of going to Barnes & Noble and seeing 5,000 copies of my book.

When I went to Barnes & Noble, I was really surprised.

First, I noticed that it was difficult to find the business section. Next, I noticed it was difficult to find the sales section within the business section.

When I found the sales section, I noticed thousands of books on selling. Mine, *Red-Hot Cold Call Selling*, was one of thousands of books on selling.

What I quickly learned was that the world did not need another book on selling—even if mine was considered to be one of the best!

I began to wonder, how I was going to differentiate myself? How was my book going to be selected over all of the other books on the shelf?

After thinking about this challenge, I realized that it was no different from the challenge we all face in our sales careers. The world probably does not need another great sales person, even if you happen to be one of the best.

19

The question we all face is what are we going to do to differentiate ourselves in a competitive market? What are we going to do to make a difference in the lives and careers of our customers? How are we going to get the market so excited about what we do that our customers and prospects line up outside of our office to buy what we are selling?

We can summarize our challenge in one question: How are we going to take our red-hot cause to market?

Most Sales Take Place after the Fifth Call

When I began to take my red-hot cause to market, I learned something very interesting. I learned that most sales take place after the fifth call. I first learned about the five-call sales cycle when I started my first business, the computer training company.

When I started the business, I was lucky enough to be the first company in a new market. Initially, I had no competition and selling was quite easy. However, when competition entered the market, I noticed that the length of my sales cycle began to increase. I noticed that it took many contacts with a customer before I would make even a small sale.

I was confused and went to a friend for some help.

She was the chairperson of a major advertising agency in New York City and received her apprenticeship in the advertising business under David Olgilvy, the founder of Olgilvy and Mather. It was my friend who taught me the power of a red-hot cause.

I told her about my new business. I complained about the competitive nature of the market and the difficulty we were having in differentiating our products and services.

She felt she could help and told me that what my business needed was a *banner*.

Since I didn't know what a banner was, she explained how she had learned about the banner concept.

She told me that when she would take an advertising program to David Olgilvy for review, he would always ask just one question. His question: "What's the banner?"

She told me that Olgilvy asked the question to see if you could identify the heart of the advertising program. He wanted to quickly understand the message you were trying to bring to market.

If you could answer the question in one sentence or less, Olgilvy would approve the program. If you could not, he sent you back to the drawing board.

My friend told me that what my business needed to be successful was a banner. She then went on to give me examples of great banners of that time.

She told me about Federal Express and its banner: When it absolutely, positively has to be there overnight.

She told me about Pepsi and its banner: For the younger generation.

And she told me about Rolaids and its banner: How do you spell relief?

We talked for a while, I told her about my business, and we soon developed a banner that I thought was great.

I ran out to find a prospect to test my new sales tool.

We sat down and I asked the prospect all of the consultative selling questions we are going to talk about later in this book. I listened to all of the answers and I took notes, just as I was taught to do in the sales programs I had taken. I was sure I was going to make a sale.

We got to the end of the meeting and the prospect asked why the company should select me, given the competitive nature of the market. I delivered my banner, my red-hot cause, and waited for the order.

Unfortunately, the prospect did not understand my banner and our meeting ended without a sale.

I went home and analyzed my performance. Maybe I had rushed into things a bit. Maybe I should have practiced.

And so I practiced integrating my banner into my sales approach until I felt I had mastered the process.

When I was ready, I called back the same prospect.

Again, I did everything right. I asked all of the questions, listened to all of the answers, and took all of the notes. With my new and improved banner, I thought for sure I would make a sale.

The moment came and so did the question: "Why should I do business with you?"

I then delivered my new and improved banner.

Unfortunately, the results were the same. No sale. This time, the prospect even seemed a little bothered by the repetition in the sales process.

After the second meeting, I went home to regroup and was greeted by my daughter, Elissa, who was two years old at the time. It was about 7:00 P.M. and my wife was preparing dinner.

Elissa came running up to me as I entered the house, gave me a big hug, and asked if she could have a cookie. Since we were getting ready for dinner, I told her she would have to wait until after dinner for her dessert.

At two years of age, Elissa demonstrated her first tendency toward a successful career in sales. She was persistent. She received her first rejection but was undaunted in the pursuit of her goal. She turned around, saw the next available prospect in the marketplace, which happened to be my wife, marched right up to her, and asked for her cookie.

Fortunately, my wife had overheard our conversation and responded in a similar manner. Elissa would have to wait.

However, Elissa was still persistent. She turned around again, came right back to me, and asked for the cookie.

It was at this point that I realized that I was selling just like Elissa. I was going back to the same customers time and time again and not adding anything new and valuable to the sales cycle.

What Elissa, at the tender age of two, realized after two trips through the sales cycle was that if she did exactly the same thing, if she approached her customers in exactly the same manner, she could expect the same results. Her great innovation was that she decided to introduce new and valuable information before her third trip through the sales cycle.

In her case, the approach was not that sophisticated. After all, she was only two years old. She simply began to cry hysterically.

But guess what?

It worked!

Both my wife and I ran to Elissa with cookies in hand.

Now you might be wondering what the moral of this story is.

I can tell you that it's not to go to your customers and start crying for the order.

Rather, each time you approach a customer, you must bring something *new and valuable* to the table. You must give your customers new reasons to meet with you, new reasons to spend some of their valuable time with you, and new reasons to buy. To do this effectively, you must have a well-developed strategy.

Since most sales take place after the fifth call, you actually need five versions of your red-hot cause in order to be successful in sales. I call these red-hot causes your company's five "unique selling points."

How to Create Your Unique Selling Points

Your unique selling points should be your company's five greatest strengths in the market. They should be developed to answer the question "Why should I do business with you?"

In order to answer this question, your unique selling points must be extremely customer-focused and have a tangible bottom-line impact on your customer's business.

Your unique selling points must also support and be consistent with your red-hot cause.

For example, as I mentioned in Chapter 1, my red-hot cause in the sales training business is:

The ₛBottom Line in Sales Performance.

My goal is to help my customers improve their sales performance by both selling more and selling more at higher prices.

As we discussed, having a red-hot cause is great. However, because most sales take place after the fifth call, we also need five unique selling points to support our red-hot cause.

So, what are my five unique selling points? How do I answer the question, "Why should I do business with you?" What gives me the opportunity to cultivate my customers and prospects until they buy from me?

The unique selling points in my business follow:

- *One-stop shopping.* I offer a full range of sales training programs, keynote speeches, and sales consulting services. This gives me the unique ability to serve all of my customer's needs in the sales performance area. The key benefit to the customer is that the company makes one purchase decision and gets consistency of application throughout its programs.
- *Real-world expertise.* Whenever I go on a sales call, I always get asked what qualifies me to teach others how to sell. I believe the answer lies in the fact that I grew my first business from zero sales to $100 million in sales in just over a decade. In addition, since entering the sales training business, I have acquired experience in

most major industries and with many market-leading organizations. Finally, I do what the sales people do. I sell. Every single day that I am not delivering a program, I am either on the telephone setting up appointments with prospects or meeting with prospects face to face. Therefore, the solutions my customers receive in my programs work!

- *Performance Plan*™. Every program I deliver is customized to meet the needs of the customer. Our proprietary customization process is called the Performance Plan™. The Performance Plan™ was developed over 15 years in the training business and is based on sound adult learning principles. The Plan combines the appropriate level of theory with practice and real-world expertise to maximize learning results.

- *Broad portfolio of offerings*. Within each of our three service lines—training, consulting, and keynote speeches—we offer a full and complete set of offerings. We offer seven fully customizable sales training programs, six keynote speeches for meetings and conferences covering the latest issues in the sales field, and a full range of consulting services, including our modular System for Selling Success™.

- *Value-based approach*. Our goal is not to deliver a sales training program. Rather, our goal is to have a tangible bottom-line impact on the customer's business. After one recent program I delivered, the sales manager said not only that this was the best sales training program he had ever attended, but also that this program would bring his group a minimum of $8,000,000 in incremental sales.

As you can see, my unique selling points not only support my red-hot cause; they also give me the opportunity to cultivate the customers and prospects in my market through more than one sales contact.

Your unique selling points should form the foundation for your entire business development strategy. Figure 2-1 demonstrates how to use your unique selling points in the sales process.

The first time you meet a customer, it's OK to introduce yourself, introduce your company, and understand the customer's needs. However, if you repeat the same process during your second and third meetings, you will start to sound redundant.

Your unique selling points give you a new point of discussion for

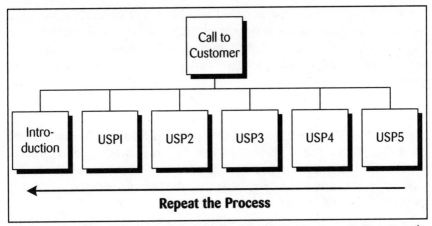

Figure 2-1. The business development cycle (USP = Unique Selling Point)

each customer contact. On your second meeting, you can focus on the first of your five unique selling points. On your third meeting, you can focus on the second of your unique selling points, and so on.

Your unique selling points system gives the customer a new reason to talk to you on the telephone, a new reason to meet with you, and—most important—a new reason to buy from you.

There are two other benefits to defining your unique selling points.

First, effective use of your unique selling points will create what I call "a Rolaids effect." I'm sure you are familiar with the Rolaids commercial, "How do you spell relief?" The answer is, of course, "R-O-L-A-I-D-S." Through repetition, an entire nation has learned how to spell relief.

If your unique selling points permeate everything you do—your letters, your telephone calls, your proposals, your face-to-face meetings, and your presentations—you, too, will create a Rolaids effect. A Rolaids effect will cause customers to come to you to gain access to your company's unique selling point offerings. In other words, you will have created your own proprietary market position.

Second, if you construct your unique selling points in a conceptual manner, you will have a business development system that will last forever.

For example, suppose that the first of your five unique selling points is that your company is consistently first to market with new products or services. Imagine that you have had six meetings with a potential customer over a period of one year and have not made a sale. A number of months ago, you presented a first-to-market product or service in an effort to do business with the prospect. Having gone through an entire sales cycle, you now have the opportunity to use the first-to-market capability again, but this time with a different angle.

The product or service that you presented as first to market one year ago is no longer first to market today. However, today, you have a new first-to-market product or service to present. In other words, you have the opportunity to present the first-to-market concept a second time and still make it sound new.

As you can see, sales are a *process*, not an *event*. In order to be successful in sales, you must learn to bet on the process. A sound process will always lead you to selling success.

How Much Time Do I Need to Invest in My Unique Selling Points?

There's a great story about a man who goes into his backyard to break a big rock. He takes a sledgehammer and hits the rock one time. The rock does not break.

He hits the rock a second time and still no results. A third strike, a tenth strike, a fiftieth strike, and a hundredth strike. The rock is still standing.

Finally, on the hundred-and-first strike, the rock breaks into little pieces and the man is left wondering which strike broke the rock.

If you were like me, you would believe that the rock broke because of the cumulative impact of the blows, not because of any one strike.

Your selling success is no different. There is no one thing you can do that will catapult you to success. It has been said that it takes 15 years to make an overnight success.

My feeling is that when you're trying to make a sale it is no different from the man hitting the rock. Your success is going to be the result of the cumulative impact of everything that you do. It will not result from any one program or idea.

In Chapter 1, we talked about your target market. Your target market is your rock.

In this chapter, we've talked about your unique selling points.

Your persistence is your hammer. Your unique selling points are the angles that you use to attack the rock.

The question we now have to address is how many strikes of the hammer will it take to break the rock? Just how much effort is required to make you a top performer? And, once you become a top performer, just how much effort will it take to keep you there?

To answer this question, you must understand where you are in the overall development of your sales career.

As we discussed in Chapter 1, there are three categories of account manager.

First, there are *new* account managers. A new account manager is one who is just starting out. Because they are just starting out, new account managers generate very little current business.

Next, there are *moderate* account managers. A moderate account manager is one who is at the fiftieth percentile in terms of sales performance. There are plenty of account managers who are doing better and plenty who are doing worse.

Please note the difference between the moderate account manager and the new account manager. New account managers are not measured based on their time on the job. New account managers are measured based on current revenue production. Therefore, if today were your first day on the job, but you inherited a territory that was generating substantial business volume, you could be in the moderate or even the top category based on the revenue production in your territory.

Finally, there are *top* account managers. We all know what a top account manager is. This is the individual who is performing at the top of his or her business or industry. We all aspire to become top account managers.

How much time you must invest in bringing your unique selling points to market is a function of where you are in your development as an account manager.

Figure 2-2 shows us that the responsibilities of an account manager or sales professional fall into one of three general categories:

- Account service
- Promoting your unique selling points
- Everything else

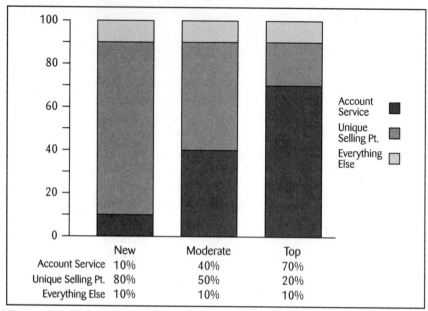

Figure 2-2. Sales time management

Account Service

Account service is any activity that you engage in relating to a customer with which you do more than $1 in business per year.

Traditional customer service would fall into this category. So would the time you spend researching or learning about your customers so that you can better serve their needs. Technical service is a third activity that would belong in this category.

Account service includes any activity you engage in that relates to a current customer. This is your first professional responsibility as a sales person and is also the easiest way to grow your business.

Promoting Your Unique Selling Points

Promoting your unique selling points is the second area of responsibility for the sales professional. To the extent that you are not servicing your customers, you should be raising the visibility of your strengths in the market.

I believe that customers will work with the company that they believe best suits their needs.

Imagine that there are 10 companies in the market, each providing a similar service. When a customer is ready to make a purchase, the decision makers will do a quick review of the potential suppliers to determine which of the 10 companies warrant further consideration. They do this on the basis of their perception of which companies best suit their company's needs.

The decision makers will then narrow their purchase decision to the two or three companies that warrant detailed consideration. Again, they will pick from among these companies on the basis of which ones best suit their needs.

Because companies are selecting the supplier that they believe best suits their needs, your job as a sales professional is to make customers and prospects understand why you are the best choice. In order to do this, you must constantly work to raise the visibility of your unique selling points in the market.

When you are not servicing your existing accounts, you should spend most of your time as a sales person raising the visibility of your unique selling points in the market.

Everything Else

After you have serviced your existing customers and after you have invested in promoting your unique selling points, you should have a small portion of your workweek left for other responsibilities. Your other responsibilities should include things like administration and paperwork.

Referring back to Figure 2-2, I have observed that paperwork and administration make up 5% to 10% of the workweek, irrespective of your category of performance. This means that you should be spending a constant two to four hours per week on paperwork and administration. If you are spending more, you may want to examine exactly what you are administering.

Please note that our estimate of two to four hours per week is based on a 40-hour workweek. In other words, you might estimate that you would spend one morning or afternoon per week on administration.

Your Investment in Your Unique Selling Points

Once you have accounted for your paperwork, your investment in your unique selling points is a function of your development level.

If you are in the new category, it is fair to say that you have very little in the way of account service. Therefore, most of your time should be promoting your unique selling points.

To make our example concrete, let us assume that we work a 40-hour workweek and spend 10% of our time on administration. Let us also assume that we spend about 10% of our time on account service. Remember: if this total seems low to you, we are assuming that you are in the new category. However, if you would like to adjust the assumption to 15% or 20%, the results will be just as striking.

If we spend 10% of our time on administration and 10% of our time on account service, we have 80% of our workweek for promoting our unique selling points. This equates to more than six hours per day (based on an eight-hour day) or four full days per week.

Figure 2-2 shows the new account manager making a substantial investment in this area. It would be safe to say that most of your efforts should be devoted to promoting your unique selling points if you are an account manager in this category.

If you are in the moderate category, your sales portfolio is characterized by a moderate number of large and developing accounts. Therefore, you will have to be spending quite a bit more time in the area of account service.

For example, assume that you are in the moderate category and are now spending 40% of your time in account service. Taking into account the 10% you still spend in administration, you still have 50% of your workweek to invest in the unique selling point process. If you do the math, you will see this amounts to four hours per day, or two and one-half days per week.

My preference in this instance is that you invest in your promotion efforts daily. If you can imagine going on a diet in an attempt to lose weight, you will probably be more successful if you diet each and every day than if you diet one or two days per week.

Likewise your promotion efforts thrive on *consistency*, not on *urgency*.

Referring back to Figure 2-2, you can see that account managers in the moderate category still make significant investments in their unique selling points. Obviously, the investments are not as significant as those made in the new category. However, they are what is required if you hope to move into the top category.

Once you have made it to the top, you still have to make consistent investments in your unique selling points. Assume that 70% of your workweek now consists of account service. Adding in the 10% constant for administration, this still leaves us with 20% of our workweek for this crucial area. This means that even those in the top category should be spending about one and one-half hours per day promoting their unique selling points. Again, consistency would be preferred over urgency.

Why Do We Need Unique Selling Points?

If you were to take a close look at a sales transaction, you would find what I consider the greatest impediment to a sale. Whenever a purchase is about to take place, the single greatest impediment is the question "Will it work?" This is obviously not the case if you are buying a single pencil, for example; however, this question permeates the mind of every buyer in a significant sales transaction.

Let's assume you are going to buy a new home. Step one in the process is that you give the seller your money. Step two in the process is that you have 30 years to see if the home works or not.

Now, of course, you do things to mitigate your risk, including having a home inspection and working with a real estate agent. However, you still bear the risk that the home might not work out to your specifications over the life of your mortgage.

Likewise, assume you go to buy a car. The circumstances are exactly the same. You give the car dealer your money and then you have the opportunity to experience the quality of the car.

Every significant transaction works in exactly the same manner. You give the supplier your money and then you have the opportunity to experience the product or service.

Customers are always asking themselves, "Will it work?" because the only certainty in a sale is the payment. The uncertainty in a sale is the big question—"Will it work?"

Customers and suppliers do a number of things in order to mitigate their risk. Suppliers offer warranties and training. Customers research the market and engage in competitive bidding.

As a sales professional, you must be in a position to convey value prior to ever working with a customer. This is where your unique selling points come in and this is why we must invest heavily in raising the visibility of our unique selling points in the market.

Customers want to know how a transaction will work prior to purchasing from us. Customers also want to know what value we can add to their sales cycle prior to entering into a relationship.

Sales people must convey safety and value to the market prior to ever making a sale.

The tools outlined in the remainder of this chapter will help you take your unique selling points to market. These tools will allow you to establish both safety and value prior to making a sale.

How to Use Your Unique Selling Points to Develop New Business

Figure 2-3 shows us some of the ways we can use our unique selling points to develop our position in the market.

The first and one of the most powerful ways to use your unique selling points is in the cold calling and telephone sales process. This process is the heart of my book, *Red-Hot Cold Call Selling*.

In addition to using your unique selling points in the telephone sales process, your unique selling points should be the driving force behind everything else you do to promote your business.

You can promote your unique selling points through a quarterly newsletter. You can also send your customers and prospects press releases, you can speak at industry conferences, you can use broadcast faxes, and you can use the Internet—all to promote your unique

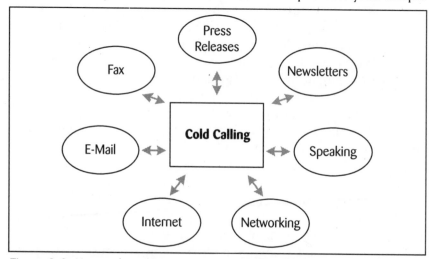

Figure 2-3. How to leverage your unique selling points

selling points. There is no limit to the number of ways you can reach out to customers and prospects in the market. Each of these supplemental strategies is discussed below.

Newsletters

One of the most powerful ways to raise the visibility of your unique selling points in the market is through a quarterly newsletter.

A quarterly newsletter gives you frequent contact with your customers and prospects.

The goals of your quarterly newsletter should be to:

- Raise the visibility of your unique selling points in the market.
- Add value to the customer's sales cycle.
- Answer the question, "Will it work?"

You can construct a newsletter that will allow you to achieve all three goals by following a simple success formula.

First, prepare your newsletter on 11" by 17" paper folded in half. This will give you four 8½" by 11" pages with which to develop your message.

Next, divide your newsletter into four sections:

- an article through which you can add value to your customers' sales cycle
- a success story
- a unique selling point section
- a direct response form

The article that you use to add value to your customers' sales cycle should be the heart of your newsletter. Remember: great sales people derive their success from the success of their customers.

This is your opportunity to make a difference. Develop one article, approximately 800 to 1,000 words, to work in this area.

Next, make use of your satisfied customers to increase your chances of success with your prospects. Develop a 500-word success story to use in the second portion of your newsletter.

Third, devote a section of your newsletter to highlighting your unique selling points.

Finally, include a direct response form so that your customers and prospects have a vehicle for contacting you.

This simple format will provide you with a powerful vehicle

through which you can communicate your message. But also remember the man and the rock. One newsletter does not a selling career make. Your success will come from *consistency* and *quality*, not *urgency*.

(Note: If you would like to be added to our free, quarterly newsletter mailing list, please send your name and mailing address to the Sales & Performance Group, 15 Sunderland Lane, Katonah, NY 10536.)

Bonus idea: A second great way to raise the visibility of your unique selling points is to take the articles that you develop for your newsletter and submit them to magazines that are important to your customers. For example, because I am in the sales training business, I submit my articles to magazines like *Selling Power, Selling,* and *Sales & Marketing Management.* I know that many of my customers and prospects read magazines like these.

Also, submit your articles to the industry publications that your customers read. If your customers are in the insurance business, they probably read *Life & Health Insurance Magazine.* If your customers are in the chemicals business, they probably read *Chemical Week.* If your customers are in either of these two industries, you should be submitting articles to these industry publications. If your customers are in other industries, you should submit your articles to the industry publications they read.

When you visit your customers, take a look at the magazines in their waiting rooms. These are the magazines they read. The publisher, editor, and the mailing address of the magazine are usually listed on the first few pages. Whenever you develop a new article, first publish it in your newsletter. Then fax it to the editor of the magazine with a cover page that says, "article submission" on it. Follow up on your fax in one month to see if the magazine is going to publish your article.

If the magazine is going to publish your article, that's great. Make certain to get a copy of the published article. You may also want to find out about ordering reprints.

If the magazine is not going to publish the article, don't worry. Most sales take place after the fifth call. Simply fax the editor the next article that you develop three months later and follow up again.

Eventually, the magazine will begin to publish your articles. A magazine editor starts each month with a lot of blank pages to fill and he or she is quite eager for quality submissions.

As you develop your list of magazine editors and as you add new editors to your list, always start the new editors at the beginning of your article list. In other words, suppose that you have been writing articles for the past three years. Since you publish your newsletter quarterly, you will have a list of 12 articles. Any time you come across a new editor, submit the first article you developed. This will give you the opportunity to send different editors different articles during the same time frame, since they will all be at different points in your cycle. It will also give you the ability to develop a series of articles for publication in the same periodical.

Double bonus: All of your articles should both be both valuable to your customers and support your five unique selling points. Because your articles will be theme-based, you may even have the opportunity to publish them in a book at some point. Many of the articles that I have written over the years have been included in either my first book and/or the book you are now reading.

Press Releases

Press releases are a third great way to raise the visibility of your position in the market and make customers and prospects excited about doing business with you. Remember that the single biggest impediment to a sale is that basic question, "Will it work?" Customers and prospects are always wondering, if they buy from you, will the transaction be successful?

One way to answer this question is to highlight your strengths in the market and show prospects how you have helped other companies just like theirs.

I issue a press release every month that I do not issue a quarterly newsletter. This means that I issue eight press releases per year. I issue my press releases only to a subset of my mailing list: those people who are either key corporate accounts or media contacts.

The press releases are intended to build your image and reputation among your key contacts. Much of the material that I use in my press releases is garnered from the publicity I get by submitting my newsletter articles to a targeted list of publication editors. However, even if you do not have a regular stream of media publicity to count on, I'm certain that you can find eight exciting and newsworthy items to use in your self-promotion over the course of a year.

Public Speaking

Speaking in public is another powerful method to raise the visibility of your strengths in the market and to get customers and prospects excited about doing business with you. In fact, I got into the business of professional speaking by speaking at industry conferences when I was in the computer training business.

When you think about it, sales professionals should love the opportunity to speak in public. If you love to sell, you should love to speak. Public speaking is simply the opportunity to sell one on *many*, as opposed to selling one on *one*.

When you speak at an industry conference, you have the opportunity to address several hundred potential customers at once. And if you're worried about a topic, your unique selling points will come to the rescue again.

When I was in the computer training business, the speech I delivered was entitled "High-Impact Training and Support." This speech was a summary of my unique selling points presented in a generic manner. The purpose of the speech was to help customers understand the key factors in working with a company like ours. In other words, I was selling one on many.

Make certain that you are speaking at the major industry conferences important to your customers and prospects. While you are speaking at these conferences, remember that most national and international industry groups have local and regional chapters as well. Make yourself available to as many groups as possible. Public speaking gives you the opportunity to reach out to many prospective customers at one time. This is in contrast to direct sales, where you must reach out to the marketplace one customer at a time.

Fax Broadcasts

Fax broadcasts are one of the most effective tools to reach out to your target market. By using a personal computer and a contact management system, any sales person has the ability to send a fax broadcast to a select subset of his or her customer base. And if you are not automated, there are service bureaus that will be happy to send the faxes for you.

There are several important points to keep in mind about fax broadcasting.

First, keep your faxes short. I try to limit my broadcast to one page whenever possible.

Second, consider broadcasting either at night or over the weekend. This is when you will have the best luck in getting through.

Please keep in mind that faxing at night is a business-to-business sales strategy. It would not be fair to fax to the home consumer market late at night.

Finally, this is a powerful communication medium. Not only do I find that people read my faxes, but also that the faxes impress them as being individual and personal. I cannot tell you how many calls I receive in response to my faxes and the messages indicate that most of the people receiving the fax actually believe that it was sent just to them.

I try to send a fax broadcast once every month to two months. You do not want to overuse this medium, since that would diminish the significance of your message.

Electronic Mail

Electronic mail is another tool that you can use to reach out to your market. I have found that e-mail is best to deliver a personal message quickly and efficiently. E-mail is a newer communication medium and its potential as a sales tool has not yet been mastered. However, I believe that electronic commerce is certainly a force of the future in sales and this is why you must start collecting and using the e-mail addresses of your customers and prospects.

Web Sites

Web sites are a must for every company. Even if you are a small company, you must have a Web site. I developed our Web site, (http://www.redhotsales.com) when we were a one-person company.

There are two keys to marketing yourself on the Web.

First, make certain that your site is registered with every search engine possible. Also make certain to use as many key words as possible so that you can attract the most visitors to your site. The key to Web marketing is to shoot broad if you are expecting your Web site to generate leads.

Second, put as many direct response forms as possible throughout your site. A Web site does not allow you to capture automatically the names of the people who visit your site. Further, I have found that "e-mail buttons" to contact your company for more information do not work as effectively as a traditional direct response form.

Summary Point

There are a number of ways you can raise the visibility of your strengths in the market. *Be creative. Be focused. Be proactive.* Whether or not you are not raising the visibility of your strengths in the marketplace, you can bet that your competition is doing it.

Are You a Great Business Developer?

Business development, or the ability to bring new business into your organization, is one of the most crucial skills for today's top sales professionals. The following seven items will test your business development acumen. These items were compiled based on years of working with market-leading sales organizations, discussions with top sales professionals, and personal experience. Take the test and see where you rank among the world's top business development specialists.

Item 1: By observing top business developers, one can rapidly conclude that selling success does not happen by accident! Today's top business developers have a very clear understanding of their target market. By clearly understanding their target market, sales professionals can focus all of their resources on the very best companies in the marketplace. By defining their target market, they have ensured that they will maximize the return they receive on the time they invest.

If you have a well-defined target market plan, similar to that outlined in Chapter 1 of this book, award yourself 5 points. If you have a partially defined market plan, award yourself 3 points. If you have a limited market plan, award yourself 1 point.

Item 2: Great business developers have also defined their red-hot cause. They have a clear understanding of their goals in the market and can summarize their red-hot cause in one short sentence.

If you have a well-defined red-hot cause, award yourself 5 points. If you have made some investment in developing your red-hot cause, award yourself 3 points. If you have made only a limited investment in developing your red-hot cause, award yourself 1 point.

Item 3: Great business developers have learned to overcome the fear of rejection. The insight here comes from the fact that they have overcome their fear of rejection not through the passing of time and the thickening of their skin, but rather from diversifying away their selling risk.

Much of your risk in sales comes from working with too few customers and prospects. Today's top business developers recognize this and have reduced their risk by working with more accounts and prospects.

Award yourself 5 points if you are completely "rejection-proof." You can tell that you are completely rejection-proof by reviewing the level of activity in your weekly planner. If your level of activity is high, award yourself 5 points. If your weekly planner shows only a moderate level of activity, you probably feel only partially rejection-proof and can award yourself 3 points. Finally, if you have only limited activity in your weekly planner, award yourself 1 point.

Item 4: Great business developers are prepared for each step in the sales cycle. They have well-developed telephone scripts, they have great, open-ended questions prepared for each sales call, and they have developed responses to common objections.

Award yourself 5 points if you have a well-developed script prepared for your telephone solicitations. Award yourself an additional 5 points if you have developed a list of five open-ended questions that you use when trying to understand customer or prospect needs. Finally, award yourself an additional 5 points if you have developed an appropriate response to the major objections you receive on your sales calls.

If you are only partially prepared in a given area, award yourself 3 points. If you feel that your preparation in an area could improve a great deal, award yourself 1 point on that portion of the question.

If you would like additional support in this area, please refer to *Red-Hot Cold Call Selling, Prospecting Techniques That Pay Off!* (AMACOM, 1995).

Item 5: Great business developers have learned how to differentiate themselves in the marketplace. They can answer the question posed by many prospects and customers, "Why pick you?"

Award yourself 1 point for each of your five unique selling points. Award yourself that point only if your unique selling point is concise and clearly differentiates you in the market.

Award yourself 1 additional point for each of the six supplemental business development strategies outlined above, up to a maximum of 5 points. In other words, if you send out a quarterly newsletter, you would earn 1 point. If you send out both a quarterly newsletter and regular fax broadcasts, you would earn 2 points.

Item 6: Today's best business developers have a clear customer focus. Earlier in this book, we presented a quotation from Dr. Norman Vincent Peale, taken from his book *How to Stay Alive All of Your Life.* Reread this quotation and determine how closely the quotation matches your selling style:

> Think first of helping Mrs. X (your customer). And to do that you must first get to know her and her family; study her needs. Do not think so much about putting her money in your pocket as putting your chair, which she needs, into her home. Do this with all of your customers. Think of them as people needing your goods instead of yourself needing their money. Find ways of helping them overcome their difficulties, and you will overcome your own in so doing.

If you feel that the magnitude of your customer focus equals or exceeds that described in the quotation, award yourself 5 points. If you believe that you are customer-focused some of the time and have an internal focus the remainder of the time, award yourself 3 points. If you believe that either you or your company have largely an internal focus, award yourself 1 point.

Item 7: Great business developers realize that their success is fully within their control. While there are clearly external factors that enter into the process, the great business developer focuses largely on things that he or she can impact. The great business developer is always moving forward.

If you believe that most of your efforts focus on areas where you can have an impact, give yourself 5 points. If you feel that your time is evenly divided between areas where you can have an impact and areas where you can't, award yourself 3 points. Finally, if most of your time is spent on areas where you can't have an impact, award yourself 1 point.

Scoring: The seven items are worth a maximum of 50 points (15 for Item 4, 5 points for each of the other six items). If you scored higher than 35, consider yourself an excellent business developer. If you scored between 20 and 35, consider yourself a good business developer, but with room for improvement. If you scored lower than 20, you have significant room for improvement on the business development front.

As we all know, business development skills, and professional sales skills in general, are learned skills. No matter how you scored in the foregoing test, there is always room for improvement. Business development is a crucial part of the sales cycle. The better you are at business development, the better you will be at selling. Look at your answers and scores on each portion of the test and determine your areas for improvement. The pursuit of sales excellence is a worthy goal.

Conclusion

Thus far, we have spent a great deal of time understanding the business development process. The business development process helps us deliver our message to the market. The business development process also helps differentiate us in the market. Finally, the business development process helps us further penetrate our existing accounts.

The next chapter will allow us to fine-tune both our business development efforts and our unique selling points by taking a much deeper look at what I consider "extreme customer focus." The next chapter will also allow us to bridge the gap between working with customers and working with prospects.

Much of what we have discussed in the book thus far has been focused on prospects. How do you get your prospects to take the first step and buy from you? As we all know, this is a formidable challenge.

The next chapter, while it will allow us to fine-tune our unique selling points and business development process, will also allow us to further penetrate our existing accounts. You clearly need new business on an ongoing basis to prosper as a sales professional, of course, but penetrating your existing accounts is the key to long-term selling success.

Chapter 3

Extreme Customer Focus

My goals in writing this book are simple. I want to help you achieve red-hot sales success. This means succeeding with two groups of people.

First, there are your prospects. How do you get your *prospects* so excited about your business that they are willing to take the first step and buy from you?

Second, there are your *customers*. How do you get your customer so excited about your performance that they are not only likely to buy again, but also to buy in increasing quantities each year?

In the introduction, we talked about making your customers successful. To me, success is the bottom line in business. Does your product or service work in the customer application?

In Chapter 1, we defined our mission or red-hot cause. Here, we talked about a customer-focused goal that would define our purpose as a sales professional.

Finally, in Chapter 2, we talked about your unique selling points and how you can bring your message to market.

We must now develop our approach one step further. Unfortunately, customers and prospects are not going to behave differently just because you read this book.

The Wizard of Oz

I'm always reminded of the final scene in *The Wizard of Oz*. The scarecrow wanted a brain and so the wizard gave him a diploma. The tin man wanted to love and so the wizard gave him a heart. The lion wanted courage and so the wizard gave him a badge.

We want to sell more.

Wouldn't it be great if customers and prospects waited outside your office in a panicked frenzy simply because you purchased this book?

Of course, but it's not quite that simple.

In order to get customers and prospects to line up to buy from us, there is one additional, crucial ingredient:

Extreme customer focus.

If you can make your customers more successful as a result of their relationship with you, they will actually wait in line to buy from you! In the words of Norman Vincent Peale,

> Find ways of helping them (the customers) overcome their difficulties, and you will overcome your own in so doing.

The key to selling success is to *make your customers successful*.

The key to selling success is *extreme customer focus*.

Extreme Customer Focus

Extreme customer focus means making your customers more successful.

However, what is *success*? How do we define *success* in business?

Success in business is simple.

Success in business means making your customers more profitable. Whenever you think about making your customers more successful, you must think about making them more profitable.

In fact, extreme customer focus means making your customers more profitable. Extreme customer focus means having a tangible bottom-line impact on the results of operations of your customers.

In Chapter 1, we told you the story of how the equipment manufacturer was able to make its customers more profitable by guaranteeing next-day parts and service with their machinery. This is a great example of extreme customer focus.

	Machine One	Machine Two
Cost	$1,000,000	$600,000
Service	Next day	Next week
Cost of downtime	$20,000/hr	$20,000/hr
Breakdowns/year	1	1
Time (maximum)	24 hours	168 hours
Cost of time	$480,000	$3,360,000
True cost	$1,480,000	$3,960,000

Figure 3-1. Illustration of extreme customer focus

If you review Figure 3-1, you can see just how the manufacturing company made its customers more profitable. The average cost of its machinery was $1,000,000. The average cost of competitive machinery was only $600,000. This is a striking $400,000 price differential—40%.

I'm not sure which machine you would buy under the circumstances; however, all other things being equal, I would purchase the lower-price machine.

Fortunately, all other things never have to be equal in sales. As Tom Peters, the great management guru, said, "Nothing need be a commodity."

I believe that great sales people differentiate themselves on the basis of the quality of their ideas. The idea that my client came up with to differentiate itself in a competitive market was next-day parts and service in an industry where the standard was next-week parts and service.

With downtime being the largest critical success factor for its customers, the company had a significant potential to save its customers money.

Figure 3-1 shows that downtime costs about $20,000 per hour in a manufacturing environment. Assuming that any piece of machinery would break down at least once per year, this one idea has the potential to save the customer approximately $2,500,000.

When we talk about extreme customer focus, we are talking about making your customers more successful. When we talk about making your customers more successful, we are talking about making your customers more profitable. When you make your customers more profitable, you must have a tangible bottom-line impact on their business.

This manufacturing example is a great example of how one company did just that.

What if I Do Not Work in a Manufacturing Environment?

The prior example was based on a company in a manufacturing environment. When your customers are operating in a manufacturing environment, the single largest critical success factor is downtime. They must keep the factories running.

However, what if your customers do not work in a manufacturing environment?

If your customers work in a service environment, you have exactly the same opportunity to make them successful.

In a factory, the largest income-producing asset is the assembly line. To make your customers successful, you may want to look to their largest income-producing asset.

In a service environment, the largest income-producing asset is the company's human resources, its people. When the head of a service company says, "Our people are our greatest asset," it's the truth, whether or not the company acts on that statement.

If your customers work in a service environment and you want to make them more successful, look to make them more productive. Look to improve the income-generating capabilities of their greatest income-producing asset.

In my computer training business, one of our largest accounts was one of the pharmaceutical giants.

While a pharmaceutical company is clearly in a manufacturing environment, our contact was the manager of computer training. Our contact's personal environment was oriented more to service than to manufacturing.

If you were familiar with the pharmaceutical business in the early 1990s, you would know that these companies were under severe cost constraints due to health care reforms proposed by the new government administration. The pharmaceutical giants were aggressively seeking new ideas to help their businesses become more cost-effective.

One of our account managers came up with the idea to save her customer, the pharmaceutical company, $2,000,000. The idea she developed was to help the customer streamline the processing of vendor invoices, which would cut costs by $2,000,000.

We learned that it cost our customer $250 to process an invoice from a company like ours. We also learned that our customer was processing 8,000 invoices per year for services similar to those that we offered.

Our account manager came up with the idea to have our customer use us as its sole source for computer training. Instead of using companies like ours in an unstructured manner, the customer would consolidate all of its purchases with one company, ours.

This may seem like a self-serving idea, but consider the benefits delivered to the customer.

If the company consolidated its training purchases with us, we could provide one invoice for computer training at the beginning of the year. The company would pay (actually, prepay) the invoice and then we would provide a monthly accounting statement.

As a result of this one idea, we were able to eliminate almost 8,000 invoices from the customer system, saving the company approximately $2,000,000. All of the cost savings resulted from making the customer more productive in the invoice-processing area.

This example should illustrate that, whether your customers are in a manufacturing environment or a service environment, your opportunities are tremendous. As a sales professional, you have an unlimited opportunity to make your customers more successful. You have an unlimited opportunity to make your customers more profitable. And you have an unlimited opportunity to differentiate your company in the market.

The Key to Your Success

The foregoing examples also illustrate that the key to your selling success is understanding the business of each of your customers.

I believe that sales people differentiate themselves on the basis of the quality of their ideas. So if you are looking to differentiate yourself in a competitive market, you are going to need a strong understanding of both the customer's business and the customer's application of your product or service in that business.

In fact, this understanding is the single greatest asset we have as sales professionals.

When you make the effort to better understand each customer's business, be aware that your understanding can grow on many fronts.

First, there is your general knowledge of the customer's business. I call this basic company knowledge. You can garner basic company knowledge by reviewing annual reports, product literature, and Web sites. It's always a good idea to have a general understanding of your customer's business.

Next, there is your knowledge of your product or service. I would consider this a prerequisite for success and believe that most sales professionals have strong capabilities in this area.

Third, there is application knowledge. Application knowledge is the first area that we can really use to differentiate ourselves. Application knowledge speaks to the premise upon which this book is built— Can you make your customer successful?

Application knowledge ensures that your product or service functions optimally in the customer environment.

There's a great story about a person selling mushrooms to large supermarket chains. This sales professional wanted to learn how his customers processed inbound shipments of his product. In other words, this sales professional wanted to ensure that his product functioned optimally in the customer environment.

What he learned was that it was very difficult to process inbound shipments of mushrooms. The workers could not stack mushrooms in a warehouse like they could most other products.

When they received a shipment of tomato cans, for example, they could stack one pallet of cans on top of another. Then, when they received the next shipment of another product, they could place that shipment on top of the tomato cans.

But they couldn't do this with mushrooms, because if they stacked something on top of a box of mushrooms, the mushrooms would get crushed.

Because the mushrooms were so delicate, the supermarket had to develop a special procedure for processing inbound shipments.

The mushrooms were placed in a special area of the warehouse. Then, the inventory manager would build a stack of pallets using other crush-proof products. Once the stack was nearing completion, the manager would take one pallet of mushrooms and place it on the very top of the stack.

The procedure prevented the mushrooms from being crushed, but this way of handling the shipments was also very costly.

Our sales professional came up with the idea of crush-proof packaging. This idea was developed based on the account manager's understanding of how the customer used his product in its business. This is also a great example of application knowledge. Application knowledge asks the question, "Does my product or service function optimally in the customer environment?" Application knowledge is one area that we can use to differentiate ourselves in a competitive market.

Industry knowledge is a second area that we can leverage to have a major impact on our customers. You can add great value for your customer by having a broad understanding of the market in which your customer operates.

For example, suppose you are doing business with Merck, the great pharmaceutical company. Suppose you are also doing business with three other pharmaceutical giants, such as Warner Lambert, Johnson & Johnson, and Pfizer.

Now suppose that you develop a fifth customer in the pharmaceutical industry. When working with your new customer, you should have the benefit of understanding "best practices" in the pharmaceutical industry by virtue of your experience with your other four customers.

This is not to imply that you should take proprietary information from one company and deliver it to others. I think that would be unethical and a highly treacherous sales strategy. However, you should have a strong idea of "how things should be done" and can use this understanding to make best practices recommendations to your other customers in the industry.

Industry knowledge can be taken even one step further.

Sometimes information and best practices that you garner in other industries, such as chemicals or retail, might be useful in the pharmaceutical industry as well.

I'm sure you've heard the old saying, "You can't see the forest for the trees." Being too close to a situation and always considering the same facts and circumstances may limit the horizons of your experiences and restrict your decision making.

Some of the challenges companies face do not vary significantly from industry to industry. For example, you can almost bet that price will come up in a selling situation, irrespective of the industry. Most industries are highly competitive and companies have a strong need to differentiate themselves in a competitive marketplace.

Be on the lookout for knowledge that you can use from one industry to make your customers in another industry more successful. The invoice processing example that we presented above would be a great example in this area.

Customers in every industry have an internal cost to process an invoice. Customers in every industry also have a strong need and desire to save money and reduce costs. This example, although it comes from the pharmaceutical business, would certainly be applicable to companies in other industries.

The Benefits of a Broad Perspective

As you study your customers, keep in mind that there are a variety of areas in which you can make an impact.

Suppose that you are selling widgets to a manufacturing company.

One way to view your relationship with your customers is strictly from a *product* perspective. You focus on one question: How can my product improve the profitability of my customer's operation? This is how most sales professionals sell.

Another way to view your customer is from a *comprehensive* perspective. A comprehensive perspective gives you a much greater ability to enhance your customer's profitability and, hence, differentiate yourself in the market.

A comprehensive view of your customer suggests that you should study your customer's business from every perspective.

If you were to review the examples I have presented so far in this book, you would see that there are many areas that we can impact as sales professionals.

The example of the manufacturing company that was able to reduce downtime for its customers is a classic example of a sales professional having an impact. He was able to make his customer's operation more effective from a manufacturing (and product) standpoint.

However, the mushroom example shows how you could also make your customer more effective from an inbound shipment perspective.

In fact, if you were to study your customers, you would find that you could divide their business into five business segments or five distinct business operations. Michael Porter, the author of *Competitive Strategy* and *The Competitive Advantage*, first proposed this method of analyzing a customer's business.

Porter suggested that any business has five distinct segments:

- The receipt of inbound shipments of raw materials
- The manufacturing process
- The shipping of finished goods to customers
- The marketing and sale of finished goods to customers
- The service of finished goods for customers

The value of this type of analysis to the sales professional is twofold.

First, it expands our view of the customer and, as a result, gives us a much greater opportunity to add value.

Most sales people focus on only one element of the customer business—the element that directly relates to the product or service that they are trying to sell.

If you were selling chemicals, for example, your tendency would be to focus on your customer's manufacturing process.

While this is a good thing to do, all of your competitors will also do the exact same thing. Because you are doing the same thing as your competitors, you will have a limited opportunity to differentiate yourself in the market and add value to the customer's sales cycle.

By looking at the five elements of a customer's business, you have four additional areas in which you can add value for an account. These four additional areas will allow you to differentiate yourself in the market.

Second, within each of the five areas listed above, you also have the opportunity to expand your view of the customer.

For example, when you look at the inbound shipments of raw materials to a customer, you naturally think about a receiving dock, the physical movement of raw materials, and the storage of raw material inventory. However, you cannot forget about the accounts payable function and the purchasing function. There is plenty of value to add in these areas as well.

Before we show you the depth of this one idea, I think it's important to note again that this model of viewing your customer applies irrespective of the line of business.

If you were working with a service company, such as a public accounting firm, the receipt function would obviously not relate to the receipt of raw materials. Rather, the receipt process in a service business is the recruitment of professional and support staff. (Remember: the income-producing asset in a service organization is its human resources.)

The manufacturing process for our service example would not be the development of finished products on an assembly line, but rather the training and development of its human resources.

The shipment of finished goods to customers would not be the delivery of a finished product but rather the delivery of its service to the market.

As you can see, our model of viewing a customer organization is quite robust and should apply to most, if not all, businesses.

The Benefits of Focus

Before we develop the specific application of the model presented above, it is also important to understand exactly what we are looking for whenever we study any element of our customer's business.

Whenever you study any element of your customer's business, you are looking for one of two things.

First, you are looking to help your customer improve the *speed* of any business process within its organization. By improving the speed of a business process, you are making your customer more productive. Making your customer more productive helps the company save time in a service environment and increase output in a production environment.

Second, you are looking to help your customers improve the *efficiency* of any business process. Our example of reducing downtime in a manufacturing environment would be a great example of an efficiency improvement.

As you review your customer's business, you are trying to help it become either more productive or more efficient. By helping your customers become either more productive or more efficient, you will clearly have a tangible bottom-line impact on their business. You will be making your customers more profitable. This is, of course, the goal of extreme customer focus.

It should be clear to you that understanding each customer's business is one of the great secrets to selling success. Most sales people simply peddle a product. You can have a significant impact on your sales results by fully understanding the application of your product or service in your customer's business environment.

This is why we presented the Porter model for thinking of any business in terms of five segments or operations:

1. Receipt
2. Manufacturing or development
3. Shipping
4. Sales and marketing
5. Service

Figure 3-2 presents your customer's business operation in a graphic format.

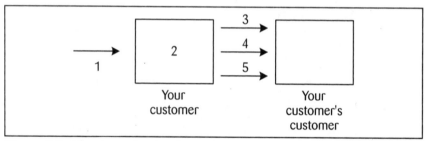

Figure 3-2. How to understand your customer

The Receipt Process

As you can see, step 1 in Figure 3-2 refers to the movement of raw materials into your customer's business.

When you review the receipt of raw materials into your customer's business, you should include any customer business process that relates, in any way, to that operation. This would include traditional business processes, such as the movement of raw materials in a manufacturing environment or the recruitment of professional staff in a service environment. But it should include non-traditional areas as well.

The more you understand your customer, the greater your benefits from using this model.

Manufacturing	Service
Receipt of raw materials	Recruitment of personnel
Accounts payable	Payroll
Purchasing	Employee benefits
Materials planning	Human resources planning
Inventory management	Human resources
Materials scheduling	Training

Figure 3-3. The receipt process

Figure 3-3 presents a number of areas that can be included in the receipt process. It is not intended to be a comprehensive list of business processes. Rather, it is provided as a beginning, to start your thinking. Your understanding of each customer's business is limited only by your desire to learn.

Of course, your desire to learn about your customer is going to be a function of your desire to succeed and excel as a sales professional, but it should also be a function of the potential value of the account.

You should make your major investments of time where the potential reward will be the greatest. And the potential reward will typically be the greatest with the larger accounts in the market. The larger accounts are where you should be investing significant time in understanding your customers' business.

This is not to imply that this model does not work for smaller customers. It applies equally well to them. However, much of your knowledge of the smaller accounts will be based on what you learn about the larger accounts.

Now that we understand the depth of the receipt process, we need to look for process improvement. Remember that the goal of extreme customer focus is to have a tangible, bottom-line impact on the customer's business. You can do this only if you are making process improvements.

Earlier in this chapter we told the story of a sales professional selling mushrooms to supermarkets. The sales person was able to help his customer improve the handling of inbound shipments of his product. This improvement saved time at the warehouse, which in turn reduced the customer's costs. In other words, the sales person had a tangible, bottom-line impact on his customer's business. This is a great example of process improvement in the receipt area.

The Manufacturing Process

The manufacturing process is probably the area that a sales person would traditionally look to for process improvements for his or her customer. The manufacturing process is represented by step 2 in Figure 3-2.

While the manufacturing process is a robust area and there is plenty of room for process improvement, keep in mind that your competitors are also looking in this area for process improvements.

You cannot be successful as a sales professional if you overlook this area, but you also cannot be successful as a sales professional if you look only at this area.

Relying solely on the manufacturing process for improvements and bottom-line impact means that you run the risk of positioning yourself as a commodity provider in a competitive market.

I would argue that you want to position yourself as other than a commodity provider.

When you consider the market position you want to occupy, you have four options relating to the delivery of your product or service. Frederick Webster, in his book, *Market Driven Management*, described the four levels of product (or service) delivery.

Webster called the first level of product delivery simply the *product*. Here, you are providing the customer with a product (or service) and absolutely no level of service or support. In effect, you are selling a commodity.

A commodity is a product or service with innumerable direct alternatives in the market. In a commodity environment, you are unable to differentiate what you are selling from the alternatives offered by your competitors.

The primary determining factor in a commodity sale is price. As you know, it is very difficult to compete on the basis of price alone.

Your second option as a sales professional is to deliver what Webster called the *expected product*. Webster described the expected product as the physical product plus the level of service and support expected by the customer.

Unfortunately, the expected product also does little to differentiate us in a competitive market. If all you are delivering is what the customer expects, you are not going to differentiate yourself from the other companies in the market that do exactly the same thing.

When your customer says, "We know you have a quality product, that's why we invited you to the meeting," the customer is telling you that you have met his or her company's expectations. Unfortunately, so have a number of other companies in the market and you are back in a commodity position.

If you want to be successful at sales, you cannot rely on an expected product to differentiate you in the market.

The third level of product delivery outlined by Webster is called the *delivered product*. The delivered product is the service level expected by the customer and something else. Here, you have in fact exceeded your customer's expectations.

However, the delivered product is still not good enough if you expect to maintain a lasting, sustainable, competitive advantage. The delivered product will allow you to maintain a competitive advantage for the short term only. Soon, your advantage will disappear and you will return to a commodity position.

Why? It's only natural. When you exceed your customer's expectations, one of two things will happen.

First, the customer's expectations may rise, in which case the delivered product will become the expected product and you will again be in a commodity position.

Second, the customer may share your idea with the market, in which case your competitors will copy your idea and the expected product will again become the delivered product.

In either event, you will again be in a commodity position and the major determining factor in a sale will be price.

If you expect to be successful in sales and if you expect to maintain a lasting, sustainable, competitive advantage, you must deliver what Webster called the *potential product*. The potential product allows you the opportunity to consistently exceed customer expectations. When you are delivering a potential product, you are many steps ahead of the competition in terms of process improvement.

In fact, process improvement and extreme customer focus become your primary sales strategy. You begin to differentiate yourself on the basis of the quality of your ideas.

Manufacturing	Service
Production	Training
Materials planning	Managing
Scheduling	Research and development
Manufacturing	Service delivery
Inventory control	Planning
Safety	MIS

Figure 3-4. The manufacturing process

The next chapter of this book will be devoted to showing you just how a sales professional can work on the potential platform. At this point it is important only to understand that we must look well beyond the obvious in our customer's business in order to be successful in implementing this type of a sales strategy.

Some business processes that are part of the manufacturing operation are presented in Figure 3-4.

Your goal is to understand how your product or service touches every aspect of the customer's business. The more you understand about your customer, the more you can differentiate yourself in a competitive market.

The more you understand about your customer, the more value you can add to its sales cycle and the greater will be the price premium you can command in the market.

The Shipment Process

The shipment process is represented by step 3 in Figure 3-2. The shipment process refers to the movement of your customer's product or service from its location to the locations of its customers.

To a large extent, the shipment process is simply the mirror image of the receipt process. When you are looking at the receipt process and your customer, you are trying to understand how you can help it streamline the process of receiving your raw materials. Your customers also have customers, and when you are looking at the shipment process, you are trying to help your customers streamline the movement of finished products from their companies to their customers.

Manufacturing	Service
Shipment of finished goods	Multiple locations
Accounts receivable	Web-based distribution
Packaging	Distance learning
Materials handling	Video-audio conferencing
Cash management	Accounts receivable
Supply chain management	Cash management

Figure 3-5. The shipment process

It should not be surprising that many of the ideas you develop to streamline the receipt process can also apply to the shipment process. In fact, almost any idea that you develop to help your customers can also be used by them to help their customer.

Figure 3-5 shows some areas that the sales professional may want to review when looking for process improvement in the shipment area for their accounts.

Remember: the goal of our account analysis is to make our customers more successful. You can measure the impact of your work on their business in three areas:

- current costs
- sales
- future costs

First, you can help your customers become more successful by helping them reduce their current costs. Much of our discussion to this point has focused on this one area.

By integrating your customers' customers into your account analysis, you should also realize that you could help your customers be more successful by helping them sell more.

For example, earlier in this book we explained how one of our account managers was able to streamline invoice processing and reduce costs for one of our customers. At first, this appears simply to be one way to help a customer reduce its current costs.

However, if you examine this idea more closely, you would see that this idea helps not only our customer, but likely its customers as well. After all, what company wouldn't want to streamline its invoice-processing costs and make its organization more profitable?

Most companies would.

The point we are trying to make here is twofold.

First, you can help your customers become more successful by helping them sell more. One easy way to do this is to show them how they can take the ideas that you have used to make their business more successful and leverage those ideas to make their customers more successful.

The second point we are trying to make here is that many of the ideas you develop will work exactly like the one we presented above. Many of the ideas in our approach to selling are not product-specific.

Since they are not product-specific, many of the ideas you develop will work irrespective of the product or service that you are selling and they will work irrespective of the product or service your customers are selling.

The implications of this concept are powerful.

First, once you develop a winning idea, you will be able to leverage that idea with most of your customers.

Second, if you take a look at where you can have an impact as a sales professional, you will find that your ideas will fall into two categories: product enhancements that help your customers become more successful and product-unrelated ideas, such as the invoice processing example presented above.

As a rule of thumb, a sales person will not have full control over product or service development within a company. In fact, a sales person may have very little influence over development. Therefore, if you are looking for areas where you can have a major impact with your accounts, you should be able to find a world of opportunities outside the product or service area.

Remember that great sales people differentiate themselves on the basis of the quality of their ideas and that great sales people are proactive in the creation of their own success.

Non-product-based strategies are a great area where you can both differentiate yourself and be extremely proactive.

The final area where you can have a measurable impact with your customers is to help them reduce future costs. Future costs are similar to current costs, except that the costs have yet to be incurred.

For example, if you are aware of new government regulations that may impact your customers, summarizing and sharing this information with them may help them avoid future costs.

Marketing and Sales

Marketing and sales are an area that sales professionals often overlook when trying to help their customers succeed. The marketing and sales operation comprises the methods and strategies used by your customers to bring their products or services to market. Marketing and sales are represented by step 4 in Figure 3-2.

When you look to this area of your customers' business, your goal is to help your customers sell more. Newsletters, technical bulletins, Web sites, and customer training can all be tremendous sources of value for your customers.

Remember to have a broad focus when you review a customer's sales and marketing efforts. You want to make certain not to overlook the obvious.

I can remember the first time I noticed that customers were asking for back issues of our newsletter. I had always thought that newsletters were a formality of the sales cycle. I never believed that my customers ever read them. I was really surprised to learn that not only did they read the newsletters, but they also considered them to be a tremendous source of value.

The Service Process

The final segment of our customers' business is the service segment. This segment is represented by step 5 in Figure 3-2. The service process is much like the sales and marketing process in that most sales people are familiar with its nuances.

The question we have to consider is this: What can we do to help our customers improve the way that they service their customers? Here, you should try to find opportunities both to increase revenues and to reduce costs.

Conclusion

Selling success does not happen by accident. Selling success is the result of a well-formed plan. Selling success is also the result of great execution. Extreme customer focus is a crucial element in your success formula.

This chapter developed a strategy through which you can implement extreme customer focus. I presented a structured process through which you can analyze your customers' businesses. The goal of this process was to add value to each customer's sales cycle and to differentiate yourself in a competitive market.

The next chapter is going to be devoted to the potential product. If you recall, the potential product provides you a means of consistently differentiating yourself on the basis of the quality of your ideas. The questions that must arise at this point are "Where are the good ideas?" and "How do I consistently differentiate myself on the basis of the quality of my ideas?"

These questions and more will be answered in the next chapter.

Chapter 4

The Potential Product

The previous chapter of this book should have made it clear that there is plenty of benefit to understanding your customer's business. The question this chapter is going to answer is "How do we leverage this understanding to increase our chances of success in the sales cycle?"

As we explained in the prior chapter, you have a choice as to how you position your product or service in the marketplace.

At one end of the spectrum, you can position your product as a *commodity*. A commodity is a product or service with many direct alternatives in the market. The major determining factor in a commodity sale is usually *price*.

What I have learned over the years is that the only way you can win as a commodity provider over the long run is to be the low-cost producer in the marketplace.

If you have ever fought the low-cost battle, you will know that it is a difficult battle to win. If there is even a single competitor that has a more efficient cost structure, you will have a difficult time maintaining this market position.

Unfortunately, if the market does not perceive you as *first* in a given category, you will have a very difficult time being successful in that category.

The Law of First

I first learned about the Law of First when I read *The 22 Immutable Laws of Marketing* by Al Reis and Jack Trout. The Law of First suggests that unless you are first in your market category, you may as well be last.

There are many popular applications of the Law of First.

For example, most of us can identify the first president of the United States. A much smaller percentage would remember the second president of the United States.

Most of us can identify the first person to fly across the Atlantic Ocean. Very few of us (including me) would remember the second person to successfully navigate the Atlantic by air.

What the Law of First suggests is that you must create a market category in which you can be No. 1.

The great Avis banner, "We're number two so we try harder," is a perfect application of the Law of First. By using this banner, Avis was conceding the number-one market position to Hertz. The company then created a category in which it could be number one— the "try harder" category.

Pepsi did the same thing with its banner, "We're for the younger/next generation." The company conceded the number-one market position to Coke. However, it also created a category where it could be No. 1.

The point we are making is that positioning yourself as a *commodity* provider is a very risky sales and marketing strategy. The reason is that, unless you are first in your market category; you will not have a long-run, sustainable position.

A better alternative in sales is to position yourself at the other end of the spectrum. A better alternative in sales is to position yourself on the *value platform*. A better alternative in sales is to deliver the potential product.

Building the Value Platform

The value platform is the platform through which you deliver the potential product. The value platform is also the platform through which you make your customers more profitable and more successful.

In fact, if you work on the value platform, your goal is not to sell as much of your product or service as you possibly can. Rather, your goal is to make your customers as profitable as you can. By helping your customers profit from their relationship with you, you will then be able to maximize the sales of your product or service. You will be deriving your success from the success of your customers.

I believe that this is the fundamental principle of business success and the fundamental principle of selling success.

When I was a young boy, I used to go to work with my parents in the summer. They were dress manufacturers: their company made dresses for sale in retail clothing stores like Bloomingdale's and Saks Fifth Avenue.

As early as I can remember, I always recall my parents talking about "reorders." Reorders were the key to success in their business.

If you are not familiar with this type of business, you may be wondering what a reorder is.

A reorder is not the initial sale of a dress to a retail outlet. Rather, a reorder takes place after the initial sale, when the store actually sells its entire inventory of your dresses to its customers. Since the store is now out of stock on this particular item, it must place an additional order with you (i.e., a reorder) to get additional units of your product to sell.

Anyone familiar with the retail business would know that a retailer does not make money when your inventory sits on the shelf. A retailer can make money only when your products sell. When your products are selling so successfully that the store must place additional orders, you are clearly making the retailer more successful and more profitable. You are achieving your goal as a successful value seller.

What my parents taught me is that if you want to be successful in business and if you want to be successful in sales, your mission must first be to make your customers successful.

You could not be successful if your goal were to sell as many dresses as possible. You could probably fool a retailer into taking your dresses for one season and maybe even two, but the retailer would notice that your dresses were not selling and would eventually stop buying from you.

Your goal can only be to sell retailers dresses that they will in turn sell. In other words, you cannot be successful unless your customers are successful.

It is for this reason that professional sales people can have one and only one goal—to derive their success from the success of the customer. If your goal is not to make your customer more successful, your career as a sales professional will be short-lived.

More on the Law of First

The reason we took the time to explain the Law of First to you is to point out that there can only be one low-cost producer in the marketplace. The Law of First tells us that if you are not the low-cost producer, you will have a great deal of difficulty competing on price.

If you cannot compete on price, then there must be an alternative. The alternative is the one we are going to develop in this chapter. The alternative is to compete on value or to deliver a potential product.

The great news is that there are infinite ways to deliver value to your customers. In other words, there are infinite ways to make your customers more successful.

Relating this back to the Law of First, there are an infinite number of categories through which you can develop a market-leading position. Remember: if you are not a leader in a category, you will have a great deal of difficulty using that category as your sales and marketing strategy.

When you compete on value, you have the opportunity to create your own market-leading categories and truly differentiate yourself in a competitive market.

How Do I Compete on Value?

The key to competing on value lies in two areas.

First, you must understand that value can be defined only in terms of your customers' profitability. When you deliver value to your customers, you make their business more profitable.

Second, you must understand that value comes in two forms: product value and non-product value.

This is a concept that we touched upon in Chapter 3. However, it warrants more in-depth discussion here.

What Is Product Value?

Product value is any value that you bring to your customer that directly relates to your product or service. Product value typically results from an enhancement to your product or service.

For example, when Intel develops its next generation of computer chips, the company will be delivering product value to its customers. Each generation of computer chip works faster than the preceding generation. By working faster, the chip should be making those people who are using the computer more productive. As you know by now, making someone more productive should result in enhanced profitability to his or her organization.

There are three issues with product value that we must consider.

First, most sales professionals are great at selling product value. If all I were going to do is write a book on product value, I doubt you would learn very much. Product value relates to the features and benefits of your product and I think most sales people know how to sell features and benefits.

Second, the advantages of product value are typically short-lived. Once you develop a product value advantage, your competitors can easily implement their version of your advantage (so as to not violate any copyrights or patents that you may have) and then add one additional product value advantage of their own.

The Intel story would support the claim that it is very difficult to maintain a long-run, sustainable, competitive advantage on product value alone unless you have a market-leading research and development organization. As we have seen with Intel, to maintain a market-leading position on product value requires that you constantly bring new product value to market. You can clearly not rest on your past product value laurels.

Finally, product value is often outside the control of the sales professional. While we may have some input into our organization's product or service design process, often the final decision is outside our area of responsibility.

In calling your attention to these three issues with product value, I do not mean to imply that product value is not worthy of consideration. It most certainly is! Our goal is to make our customers more profitable and I would support any legal and ethical strategy in this area.

The only word of caution I wish to offer at this point is that I do not believe it's a good idea to place all of your eggs in the product value basket. It pays to consider the non-product aspect of your customer relationship as well—especially since this area actually offers the sales professional quite a bit more potential than the product value area.

What Is Non-Product Value?

Non-product value is any value that you bring to your customer that does not specifically relate to your product or service. Typically, non-product value will take the form of an idea or strategy. It's any idea or strategy that you bring to the table as part of your in-depth knowledge of the account that makes that customer more successful.

In Chapter 3, we developed a process for analyzing your customer's business. We said that any customer's business could be divided into five distinct categories:

- The receipt of inbound shipments of raw materials
- The manufacturing process
- The shipping of finished goods to customers
- The marketing and sale of finished goods to customers
- The service of finished goods for customers

In this chapter, I would like to develop a process for delivering non-product value.

You can deliver non-product value in any or all of five ways:

- Business know-how
- Supply chain optimization
- Operational support
- Ease of doing business
- Organizational strength

Business Know-How

Business know-how is perhaps one of the richest sources of value for the sales professional. Business know-how allows you to take your general business knowledge and apply it to a specific customer to make that customer more successful and more profitable.

There are many good examples of business know-how that I can share with you. I'll take a moment to summarize just a few.

One of my customers is a world-class chemical giant. One of the things this company is known for is world-class technical support. When you buy chemicals (a commodity) from this company, you also get access to its world-class technical service organization to help you implement its product in your production process.

You might imagine that world-class technical support is a great source of value to this company's customers—and it certainly is. However, if you were to put technical support into one of the five categories listed above, it would more commonly fall into the "Operational Support" category.

The reason I am telling you about this aspect of its business here is because this company took its technical service operations one step further.

Remember that there could be other world-class chemical companies offering excellent technical support to their customers. So other questions then arise. How do you raise the bar? How do you differentiate yourself in a competitive market? How do you deliver a potential product? How do you do something that your competition is not also doing?

This company knew that world-class technical support was one of its unique selling points and contributed greatly to its success. However, this company also knew that competitors could also deliver world-class technical support.

So the company gave its customers the opportunity to deliver world-class technical support to their customers. When you worked with my customer, not only did you get a great product and great technical support, you also got training in technical support delivery so that you could implement a world-class technical support organization within your company. Then, once you had a world-class technical support organization within your company, you could in turn deliver world-class technical support to your customers.

It should be easy to understand how this type of training and this type of offering should help that world-class company enhance the profitability of its customers.

What if I Don't Work for a Large Company?

The prior example showed how a large organization, with its vast resources, can enhance the profitability of its customers. So you may be wondering, "Will this type of process work for me if I don't work in a large company?"

The answer to this question is obviously yes. You can be a great source of value for your customers irrespective of your company size.

One of my customers once gave me a call and asked if I could deliver a marketing program for her company. Unfortunately, I do not deliver marketing programs. I could have ended the conversation at this point; however, I elected to add value into my customer's sales cycle.

Instead of just thanking her for thinking of me, I gave her referrals to three companies that I had worked with. All three of these companies deliver excellent marketing programs.

You might think this is a simple idea and hence not worthy of discussion. However, let's take a deeper look into what I did.

The customer called me assuming that I could easily deliver the program. I would guess that her estimate of the time it would take to select a provider was minimal. Unfortunately, I did not have the capacity to deliver the program, which caused an unexpected change in plans.

If I had not given the customer those referrals, she would have had to do some research to generate three leads on her own. Since she was not familiar with the new companies in question, she would have also had to travel to view programs offered by each of them.

The company was looking for a two-day program and she would also have had to invest one travel day per program review. That meant that she would have invested three days (one travel day and two program review days) for each of the three companies, plus upfront research time of one-half day and then one-half day to summarize her results. I estimate that my referral saved the customer ten days' worth of work. The time saved might have been greater had the company gotten a second decision maker involved in the vendor selection, as is often the case in large companies.

Sources of value are all around us. There are complex sources of value, such as the one delivered by the chemical company. There are less sophisticated sources of value, such as the information I provided to my customer. However, in the final analysis, value is value. In both instances, the sales professional was able to save his or her customers money. In both instances, the sales professional was able to make his or her customer more profitable. In both instances, the sales professional had a tangible bottom-line impact on his or her customer.

Paul's Rule of One

One of the comments I always get in my seminars at this point is that the examples I've just presented are great. However, they could easily be copied by the competition.

While this may be true, one of the key learning points of this book is that you should never bring just one source of value to your customers. Paul's Rule of One tells us that anytime there is only one variable involved in a sale, the sales person stands a great chance of losing.

If you bring only one value idea to the customers, they may tell you that your idea is great, but will simply not work in their business. They may also tell you that your idea is great and they will place it out to competitive bid. In either case, you will lose.

When you work with your customers, you must understand that adding value is a *process*, not an *event*. You must always look for ways to make your customers more successful.

If you review Figure 4-1 on the next page, you see that if all you are going to bring to your customers is a commodity (1), you are playing directly into their hands. The major differentiating factor in a commodity sale will usually be price.

However, if you bring one value idea to the table along with your product or service (2), you begin to change the composition of your offering. But there's a problem with putting only one value idea on the table—at best you stand only a 50/50 chance of being successful.

As noted above, the customers may tell you your idea will not work in their environment or the customers may share your idea with the market.

If you bring a second value idea to the customers, you continue the differentiation process. A third value idea (3) adds to the differentiation process. A fourth idea (4) takes the process one step further.

The more value you add to the customers' sales cycle, the more you will differentiate yourself in a competitive market.

The more value you add to the customers' sales cycle, the more difficult it will be for the customers to take your ideas to market for competitive bid.

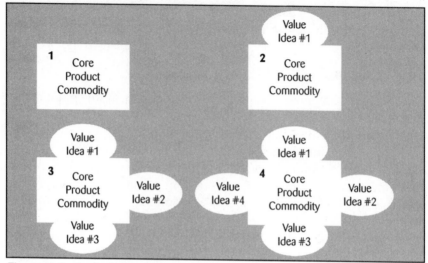

Figure 4-1. Paul's Rule of One

The more value you add to the customers' sales cycle, the more difficult it will be for the competition to copy your offering. You will, in effect, be building barriers to entry into your account.

Finally, the more value you add to the customers' sales cycle, the more unique your product or service will be. And as you bring a unique product or service to the market, you begin to control the market price for your product or service.

The bottom-line message here is that adding value must be a way of life. Adding value into your customers' sales cycles must be your sales philosophy. And the good news is there is no limit on the amount of value you can add to your customers' sales cycle.

Back to Business Know-How

Business know-how refers to the knowledge that you can bring to your customer that will help your customer become more profitable as a result of its relationship with you. I believe that this is one of the most powerful sales tools available to us as sales professionals.

Business know-how can come from many sources. You can get it from studying your customers in the manner we suggested in Chapter 3. You can also get it from annual reports, Web sites, and company brochures.

Additional sources might be your knowledge of the customer account, your knowledge of the customer industry, or your knowledge of other industries that may face similar challenges.

You can also build your business know-how by reading general information resources such as *The Wall Street Journal, USA Today,* or industry publications. I would find it hard to imagine that a day could go by without one of these three sources providing you with information that may be important to your customers.

Figure 4-2 presents some potential sources of value in the business know-how area. This list is not comprehensive; it is only meant to get you started.

- Materials handling seminars
- Training videos
- Technical service
- Cycle time improvement
- Newsletters
- Sales leads
- Market information
- Supply/demand information
- Changes in regulatory climate
- Training programs
- Changes in the political climate
- New government regulations
- Business advice
- Technical bulletins

Figure 4-2. Business know-how

Great sales people differentiate themselves on the basis of the quality of their ideas and it will be up to you to add items to the list. If all you are going to do is bring the same ideas to the customer as your competitors, you will do little to differentiate yourself in a competitive market.

Supply Chain Optimization

Supply chain optimization is the second non-product source of value that we can bring to our customers.

Supply chain optimization asks the question, "What can we do as sales professionals to reduce inventory carrying costs in a manufacturing environment?" Supply chain optimization also asks, "What can we do to save our customers time in a service environment?"

In both circumstances, we are obviously referring to the delivery of either products or services into our customers' business or the shipment of products or services out of our customers' business.

My favorite example of supply chain optimization came when I began my speaking career. I went to visit a new account to learn about the business. This was a manufacturing company and one of the things I did was tour the assembly line.

As I began to walk "the line," I noticed that there was a basket of screws at each point in the assembly line where a piece was added to the end product. This would probably not be exciting to you, but it was really exciting to me.

The reason it was exciting to me was that my brother-in-law was in the screw business. He was a screw distributor.

The company I was working with was the largest of its kind in the world. I began to think not only about my speech but also about landing a world-class account for my brother-in-law.

I asked the obvious question, "Where do you buy your screws?" My account contact said, "That's an interesting question."

I wondered what could be so interesting about a question like that, but he went on to tell me.

He explained that the company had been buying screws from the same account for as long as he could remember, and he had been at the company for almost 20 years.

I was surprised at the level of loyalty to a supplier of products and services, especially one involved in the distribution of screws.

He then told me why.

He pointed back to the baskets of screws that had caught my attention. He told me that each night the supplier would send in a team of people to review production records and then make certain that there would be a sufficient supply of screws on hand in each basket for the next day's product run.

He then pointed to another area in the facility and told me about the vendor-managed inventory. He said that the inventory there belonged to the supplier, which eliminated inventory-carrying costs for my customer. He also told me that the team of people made certain that there was sufficient inventory on hand to ensure that there would never be a production stoppage.

It started to become clear to me why the customer had never changed supplier. The value ideas delivered by the supplier included the following:

- Vendor-managed inventory on the assembly line
- Vendor-managed inventory in the warehouse
- Billing for exact usage only
- Elimination of downtime due to inventory shortages
- Elimination of computer systems to manage the inventory
- Elimination of personnel to plan, manage, and distribute the inventory
- Elimination of scrap and waste

The value brought to the relationship by this supplier, in this one area alone, probably far exceeded the cost of the products provided to my customer.

Before we move from the topic of supply chain optimization, we must make two additional points.

First, it is important to note that supply chain optimization works just as well in a service environment.

My computer training business developed a network of locations so clients could take computer-training programs near their offices or their homes. The benefit to the customer was to minimize travel time to a program. We called this program our Corporate Account Plan and were very successful at selling this source of supply chain value to the market.

Second, if you were to analyze your customer's balance sheet, you would find that it has four significant asset categories: cash, accounts receivable, inventory, and fixed assets. When you are running a business, it is usually a good idea to increase your cash balances and, at the same time, keep your accounts receivable and inventory to a minimum.

As you are well aware, cash is the commodity of purchase in our economy. Without cash, companies will not be able to make the investments required to grow their business.

Accounts receivable and inventory are the business antithesis of cash. To the extent that you have more accounts receivable or more inventory, you tend to have less cash. Any value recommendation that would decrease accounts receivable and/or inventory would tend to increase cash.

Supply chain is one value area in which ideas can directly reduce inventory balances and hence increase cash balances. As you will see in the next chapter, any idea that both reduces inventory balances or accounts receivable balances and increases cash can have a major impact on the profitability of your customers.

Figure 4-3 is intended to stimulate some thought on value solutions in the supply chain area.

> - Supply chain management
> - Channel strategy
> - Optimum packaging
> - Consignment inventory
> - Warehousing
> - Equipment design
> - Plant/office design
> - Materials handling consulting
> - Emergency shipments
> - Emergency technical service
> - One-stop shopping
> - Lost inventory
> - Inventory management
> - Reduced routing times
> - Just-in-time inventory
> - Reusable packaging

Figure 4-3. Supply chain optimization

Operational Support

Operational support is the third non-product source of value you can bring to your customer. Operational support typically looks more to your resources as an organization than to your expertise as a sales professional.

Operational support asks the question, "What time, tools, people, or capital can we bundle with our product or service offering to improve customer profitability?"

The good news is that you are probably delivering operational support as part of your product or service offering every single day. Operational support can be as simple as extended credit terms for your customers. If you are providing extended credit terms, your customers do not need to go to a bank or other funding source for credit.

Operational support can also take the form of technical support that we all provide to our customers, through the technical service representatives of our organizations or on our own as sales professionals.

Operational support can also take the form of consignment inventory or financing that you provide to your customers for construction projects or capital equipment.

Operational support is any time, tools, people, or capital that you provide to your customers as part of your product or service offering to help the customer become more successful and profitable.

By way of example, one of my customers is a company that manufactures home improvement products. It sells its products to companies like Home Depot, Scottie's, Menard's, and other home im-provement centers.

As part of its overall product offering, this company assigns a sales person to provide support whenever the customer opens a new store. The sales person is responsible for product merchandising (i.e., displaying the company's products as attractively as possible on the store shelves), on-the-job training, and technical support to facilitate the store opening.

Clearly, this type of resource would help make the customers more profitable by making store openings more effective.

Figure 4-4 provides you with a sampling of ideas in the operational support area.

If I were to guess your reaction after reviewing Figure 4-4, I would assume that you already deliver many of the items listed. I would also assume that your competition might also deliver some of the items listed.

There are two important points that we need to make here.

First, I want to remind you that great sales people differentiate themselves on the basis of the quality of their ideas. Bill Gates, when he formed Microsoft, did not go out and copy what all of the other companies were doing. He did something different.

Your job is not to copy what the other sales professionals are

- Value audits
- Plant audits
- Business audits
- Accounts receivable/payable options
- Equipment financing
- Customized billing procedures
- Training programs
- Technical service
- Equipment service
- Laboratory services
- In-house process capabilities
- Environmental services
- On-the-job training
- Equipment loans
- Facility loans
- Receivables financing

Figure 4-4. Operational support

doing. You job is first to determine each customer's needs and then to provide a solution to those needs that differentiates you in a competitive market.

It is your job to "raise the bar" beyond what is presented in Figure 4-4. My job is to teach you the concepts.

Second, remember that selling is the successful management of customer perceptions about what is important in a relationship. It is your job to communicate the value you bring to each customer's business organization.

One of the most common mistakes I believe that we all make as sales professionals is to constantly deliver value to our customers.

But why is that a mistake?

Good question! The problem lies in the fact that we often don't take the time to quantify the value we deliver (which is the topic of the next chapter) and we rarely take the time to communicate our success to the customer (which we will cover in a later chapter).

Ease of Doing Business

Ease of doing business is the fourth area of non-product value for the sales professional.

I first came across this idea when I was working in my first business, the computer training company.

We wondered what were the major decision-making points when our customers made a purchase decision. We hired an independent organization to survey the major buyers in our marketplace.

We were selling to *Fortune* 2000 companies and we developed a list of 20 vendor-selection criteria. Among the criteria were items such as the price of the product, product quality, delivery, payment terms, training, warranty, and ease of doing business.

The independent organization took the list of 20 criteria to our target market and asked the survey participants to rank the criteria in terms of importance to their vendor-selection process.

Most sales professionals would probably think that price was the major criterion for selecting vendors. I know that's what we thought—prior to the survey.

Most sales professionals would also believe that criteria such as product quality, payment terms, and product delivery would also rate high in vendor selection. I know that's what *we* thought—prior to the survey.

We were surprised to learn that the number one vendor selection criterion in our business (computer training) was *ease of doing business*. Our customers and prospects did not want to spend a lot of time processing our invoices and placing orders with us.

Rather, they wanted to spend most of their time servicing their customers. They felt that the only way they could do this was if it were easy to do business with their suppliers.

Now you may not be in the computer training business and you may not sell to *Fortune* 2000 companies. However, the point I am trying to make by sharing the results of this survey with you is not that ease of doing business will always be the most important vendor-selection criterion for your customers. Rather, the point is that this area of value has a lot of potential for us as sales professionals.

Ease of doing business may not be the first vendor-selection criterion for your customers, but I can guarantee you it will not be the last.

My most significant experience with ease of doing business came with my computer training company. We finally succeeded in winning a major customer away from one of our largest competitors.

The competitor had a firm grip on the account for many years, until one of our account managers came up with a brilliant idea on how to properly position us with the customer. I am not going to tell you the idea at this point, since it is the focus of Chapter 6.

However, needless to say, her strategy was tremendous and we stole a major account from one of our largest competitors.

After we celebrated our success, we soon noticed that our new customer was paying our bills in 90 days or more. It does not take a lot of business acumen to understand that if you are paying your bills in 30 days and getting paid by your customers in 90 days, you will not stay in business very long.

After a while, we were getting so frustrated with the account that we almost wanted to give it back to the competitor. We felt we could do more damage to our rival by letting it have an account like this than we could by keeping the account!

Finally, in utter frustration, we visited the customer and asked somebody there why the company could not pay our bills on time. After all, it was a large, venerable organization. It was an institution in the marketplace. The magnitude of our bills could clearly not place its cash flow in jeopardy.

What I was about to learn was one of the most eye-opening business experiences I ever had.

The person was unsure why the company was not paying our bills on time either. He knew, however, that the company was not happy with its new relationship. The people felt the company was investing too many resources in paying our invoices, investing too much in the administrative aspect of our business relationship.

In short, it was not easy to do business with us!

As we investigated the situation further, we learned that our account manager was so excited about her victory that she had neglected to set up a good operational process. Our account manager completely forgot about the administrative aspect of our relationship with the customer.

As we began to examine our business practices, we learned that this was a common occurrence. Most account managers are so happy when they win a sale that they forget to establish a strong operational process with the customer. They completely neglect the ongoing portion of their relationship with the customer.

However, as you will see when we finish the story, there is great value in creating a strong operational process. There is great value in making it easy to do business with you.

What we did in this instance was to get our accounting staff together with the customer's accounting staff. Both teams spent time to understand the operational process between our businesses and both teams went to great lengths to establish a set of win/win procedures.

The solution they developed was for us to submit our invoices to the company electronically and for the company to pay our invoices via electronic funds transfers. They were able to cut a 90-day payment cycle down to five business days.

Obviously, we were thrilled to death. But so was the customer. The company was now able to take the resources it had committed to our accounts receivable process and invest them in more important business functions. The company was now able to focus its efforts on serving its customers.

In fact, the people there were so happy with the solution that they stated that they would never stop doing business with us! And they made this statement not because of the high quality of our product, but because of the strong operational process that we had created.

Figure 4-5 provides you with a sampling of value-based ideas in this area.

- Electronic data interchange
- Customized procedures
- Electronic mail interchange
- Electronic order processing
- Electronic bill payment
- Customized billing procedures
- Fax on demand service
- Video conferencing
- ISO certification
- Trouble-free process
- Customized invoice formats
- Special delivery requirements
- Electronic inventory management

Figure 4-5. Ease of doing business

Organizational Strength

Recently my mother retired from a 40-plus-year career as a sales professional. Since I am always trying to grow and learn as a sales professional, I went to my mom and asked for advice.

I wanted to know what one thing she had learned above all others after 40 years in the field. Here's what she said:

> The one thing I've learned after all these years in the field is that the customer always gives you the roadmap to success. The problem is that most sales people are too busy trying to impress the customer with how good they are, how good their company is, and how good their product is to ever listen to what that roadmap is!

The reason I tell you this story is because too often our sales approach focuses on trying to impress the customer.

How often have you heard a sales person tell the customer, "My company is the *largest* in the business"? How often have you heard a sales person tell the customer, "My company is the *oldest* in the business"?

Whether your company is the oldest or largest is not what's important to your customers. What's important to your customers is the *value* they derive from your strong market position.

For example, one of my customers is an environmental services organization traded on the New York Stock Exchange. The company cleans factories, paper mills, power plants, and oil refineries so that its customers can continue to operate their businesses.

One issue they face is that many of the other environmental services companies are smaller, "mom and pop" type organizations. The smaller organizations have a different cost structure and can often offer a similar service at a lower price.

At first glance, you might believe that these smaller organizations have a competitive advantage based on their size and cost structure. And they may—at first glance.

However, perhaps the single largest issue in the environmental services business is safety. When an accident occurs in a factory, a power plant, an oil refinery, or a paper mill, people often lose limbs or even lives.

As you can imagine, litigation surrounding the loss of limbs or lives can be very costly. This is why my client maintains its insurance with a triple-A-rated insurance firm. Smaller competitors cannot afford the insurance premiums charged by the larger insurers and they tend to use smaller, less reputable firms.

Now this may not seem important to a customer in this industry. Not important, that is, unless there's an accident. Unfortunately, accidents are part of the environmental services business and companies must consider that fact of life when they select vendors.

The value to the customer in this instance is that, if an accident occurs, my client's insurance company will pay the claim. Smaller organizations and smaller insurance providers have been known to have inadequate resources to meet similar claims. My client has a competitive advantage in that the customer knows that my client will honor insurance claims.

Examples of organizational strength include size, years in business, the ability to honor insurance claims and warranties, a global distribution system, and applications expertise.

However, as sales professionals, we cannot stop here. We must always take these strengths and translate them to ideas that have a tangible bottom-line impact on the results of operations of our customers.

Product or Service Design

The final source of value that we are going to discuss in this chapter is the design of your product or service. This could be a new feature of your product or it could be a new design or packaging idea for your product.

This is the most obvious source of value and the one that most sales people are adept at presenting to their customers. In the old school of selling, this was known as "features and benefits" selling: we place a new feature on our product and sell you the benefit of using the new feature.

The problem with features and benefits selling alone is threefold.

First, most sales people are adept at selling features and benefits. Therefore, features and benefits selling alone will do little to differentiate you in a competitive market.

Second, product features or enhancements are easily copied by the competition. When I add a feature to my widget, competitors will find out. They will then copy my feature and add a new feature of

Chapter 5

What's in This for Me?

You may well be wondering at this point, "What's in this for me?" So far in this book, we have spent all of our efforts making the customer successful. Although I believe this is the essence of successful selling, there must also be a win for us, the sales professionals. Not only must there be a win for us, there must also be a win for our organizations.

If the strategies outlined in this book are not going to make us more successful, there is really no point in executing them.

However, these strategies will indeed make us more successful. The keys to your success lie within this chapter.

But before we learn about these keys, I want to take a few moments to elaborate on what we have discussed thus far.

Using any of the ideas presented in this book will raise your level of success as a sales person. However, using them all together will raise your level of success much, much more. I wanted to take a moment to show you how you can put together all the ideas in this book to really make your sales career red-hot!

The Potential Product

In Chapter 4, we introduced the potential product. The potential product was the actual product or service sold by your company and all of the value ideas you could add to the product.

Chapter 4 also showed us that there are six categories of value:

- Business know-how
- Supply chain optimization
- Operational support
- Ease of doing business
- Organizational strength
- Product or service design

After reading Chapter 4, you should understand that there are really unlimited opportunities to deliver value to your customer. Within each category of value, there is no limit to the ideas you can generate. Your potential for adding value is limited only by your sales acumen, your imagination, and your desire to be successful.

The six categories of value are clearly a powerful concept. However, we can leverage the power of this concept by combining the ideas presented in Chapter 4 with those of Chapter 3.

Chapter 3 gave us a structured process for understanding our customer's business. This model was based on work done by Michael Porter.

Porter's model suggests that any business can be divided into five distinct segments:

- The receipt of inbound shipments of raw materials
- The manufacturing process
- The shipping of finished goods to customers
- The marketing and sale of finished goods to customers
- The service of finished goods for customers

The leverage comes from the fact that you can use the six categories of value to add value to any one of the five segments of a customer's business.

For example, suppose that you are trying to better understand your customer's receipt process. By using the six categories of value with this one segment of your customer's business, you now have five new areas of value that you can add to your customer's sales cycle.

First, you could use your business know-how to enhance the profitability of your customer in terms of its receipts process.

You could also use your knowledge of supply chain optimization to improve the customer's receipt of raw materials.

In fact, in order to fully explore your customer's receipt process, you need to ask yourself the following six questions:

1. *Know-how*. What information do I have that can add value to my customer's receipt process?
2. *Supply chain*. How can I help my customer optimize its receipt of raw materials?
3. *Operational support*. What resources can I provide to my customer to make its receipt of raw materials more cost-effective?
4. *Ease of doing business*. How can I make it easier for my customer to process the receipt of raw materials?
5. *Organizational strength*. How can I leverage the strengths of my organization to make my customer's receipt process more successful?
6. *Product design*. How can I design my product to make processing of inbound shipments more effective?

In fact, if you think about it, you should be able to ask similar questions for each of the remaining four business processes.

The purpose of this discussion is to highlight that there are really 30 ways to add value to your customer's sales cycle—using the six areas of value to make your customer more successful in each of its five business processes.

And there are still an infinite number of applications within each category. Therefore, you are again limited only by your business acumen, your imagination, and your desire to make your customers (and yourself) more successful.

Before we move beyond our focus on making your customers more successful, I should point out that your customers also have customers. Therefore, any idea that creates value for your customers may have potential for them to use to create value with their customers.

Remember: we can add value for our customers by reducing their costs, either current or future. The 30 categories of value discussed thus far largely relate to the opportunity to save your customers money.

However, we can also add value for our customers by helping them sell more. This is where understanding that your customers also have customers has a major impact on your chances for success in the sales cycle.

By understanding that your customers have customers, you should also understand that any idea that saves *your* customers money might also save *their* customers money. If *your* customers can save *their* customers money, they will be making *their* customers more successful.

If *your* customers can make *their* customers more successful, their customers will likely buy more from them (the whole premise of this book) and thus increase their revenues. In other words, by helping your customers help their customers, you will help them sell more. This adds value to their sales cycle and increases your chances of success with your customers as well.

If you follow the tack I am taking, you will understand that there are really 60 questions you could be asking, not just the 30 questions outlined above. The first 30 questions can be used to add value for your customers and the second 30 questions can be used to help your customers add value for their customers.

True sales professionals will always take their analysis this additional step, so they can understand how to make their customers more successful from a revenue perspective as well.

There is one final point I would like to make on this concept of making your customers more successful from a revenue perspective.

There are industries where you can take our revenue analysis to a third, fourth, and possibly even fifth level. Just as your customers have customers, so too do their customers have customers. This process can be followed until you reach the final consumers of a product or service. And because we can follow this process through a value chain, we can add value as far up the value chain as we would like.

As long as you can identify an area of impact for your product, service, or ideas, there is no limit to the extent of your revenue analysis. However, please keep in mind that the further your analysis progresses away from your business, the less likely you will be able to make a significant impact.

Your Unique Selling Points

The concept of delivering value to your customers presented in Chapter 4 and the concept of your company's five unique selling points presented in Chapter 2 are also highly interrelated.

Your unique selling points were designed to motivate prospects to take the first step and buy from you.

When you analyze the process of building a relationship with a prospect, I believe that the first step is the most crucial in the process.

Most existing customer relationships are stable. A stable relationship is one in which the customer has already satisfied its need for a product or service and is happy with its relationship with the vendor.

Therefore, if you are calling on a prospect, you can assume that that company is already using a product or service similar to yours and is happy with the vendor.

If the company were not happy with the vendor, it did not have to wait for your call to make a change. This is something the company could clearly have done on its own. By the time you called, the company would have already replaced its current provider with a new one.

This is not to imply that you will not come across situations where the prospect is right at the point of making a change. You will. We all have. However, I do not believe this should be the basis of your sales strategy. Rather, I would like to install a process for motivating prospects to make the first step and buy from you. Your unique selling points and your core/niche selling strategy are designed to be these motivating factors.

Your Core/Niche Strategy

The core/niche account penetration strategy starts with understanding the difference between a *core* business opportunity and a *niche* business opportunity.

A *core* business opportunity is that portion of a customer's needs for which solutions are readily available on the open market. You could supply a great core solution to the customer—and so could most of your competitors.

Unfortunately, because core business opportunities are readily available in the open market, core business tends to be commodity-oriented and very price-sensitive. When a customer starts negotiating with you about the price of a product or service, the company is really referring to the core business. Looking at it from another perspective, we have not done a good enough job as sales professionals to shift the focus from core business to niche business.

Niche business, on the other hand, is that portion of a customer's needs for which solutions are not readily available in the open market. Because niche solutions are not readily available in the open market, and because the customer *needs* the niche idea, product, or service, niche business opportunities can go a long way to differentiate you in a competitive market. Niche business, because it is not readily available in the open market, also tends to be much less price-sensitive.

Figure 5-1 presents the core/niche account penetration strategy in graphic terms.

When most sales people sell, they sell directly to the core business opportunity, the portion of a customer's needs for which solutions are readily available in the open market.

Also, because core business is readily available in the open market, core business tends to be very price-sensitive. When you sell directly to the core, the major differentiating factor is usually price.

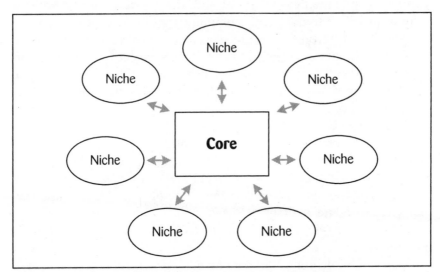

Figure 5-1. The core/niche account penetration strategy

The most common way to wrest core business from the competition is to lower your price.

As you know, lowering your price is not the most effective long-run business strategy. Lowering your price will have an adverse impact on the profitability of your company and this is something that we all must be concerned with over the long run.

An alternative to selling to the core is to sell to the niche, the portion of a customer's needs for which solutions are not readily available in the open market. Niche business is something the customer needs but does not have. Niche business opportunities are the value-selling ideas that we were referring to in Chapter 4.

The most effective way to penetrate the prospects in the market is by providing something that they need, yet do not already have. And this is what your unique selling points are designed to do.

Your unique selling points can help you bring your value message to market. In Chapter 4 we developed the multitude of value ideas that you could deliver. Your unique selling points should be your five greatest strengths in the market. Your unique selling points should be your five greatest value ideas from Chapter 4.

In fact, if you take the time to develop the ideas presented in Chapter 4, you will find that many of the ideas will fall into similar categories. It is the five categories with the greatest impact that you may want to use to craft your company's five unique selling points.

Specifically, I would review the six categories of value as they relate to each of the five segments of a customer's business. I would try to develop as many ideas and potential ideas as I could for each category.

Assuming that you have done this, you may have five applications of the value concept for each of the 30 categories of value described above.

Once you have developed the applications of value (in this example we would have 150 value applications, using five applications for each of the 30 categories), you should review them for consistency.

For example, you might find that a number of the 150 applications really relate to your position as a global organization. You would then use "global organization" as one of your five unique selling points.

You might also find that a number of other applications related to your strong research and development capabilities. You would then use your research and development expertise as the second of your five unique selling points.

In essence, your unique selling points should serve as a summary of your greatest value points. If you develop your unique selling points in this manner, you will have a consistent message that you deliver to the market from one end of the sales cycle (i.e., your prospects) to the other (i.e., your major accounts).

Your Red-Hot Cause

Your red-hot cause should be the summary of your five unique selling points and should be a one-sentence statement of your mission as a sales professional.

This book has been devoted to showing you how to derive your success as a sales professional from the success of your customers. Therefore, your red-hot cause should relate to the role that we have been advocating throughout this book.

One of my customers, the Dow Chemical Company, had a great red-hot cause along these lines:

We Don't Succeed Unless You Succeed!

Another of my customers, Allwaste Environmental Services, had another great red-hot cause along these lines:

Helping Our Customers Become More
Competitive in a Global Environment

You see, making your customers more successful and implementing the ideas in this book are not something that you can do on a part-time basis. What we are advocating within this book is a *selling lifestyle*.

And because we are advocating a selling lifestyle, it is crucial that everything that you do in your sales career drive directly through the point of making your customers more successful.

Building Success on Success

Now that we have seen how the ideas in this book work together, let's take a look at how we can derive our success from the success of our customers.

Suppose you're selling widgets. And suppose the cost of your widget is $1. A competitor is selling similar widgets for $.90. While the $.10 price differential may not seem significant to you, the customer is about to place a large order—one million widgets, to be exact.

If you take the $.10 differential and multiply it by the number of units in the order, the customer will be spending $100,000 more with your company. Times are tough and the customer is having trouble justifying your higher cost.

I'm sure you've heard the old saying, "A penny saved is a penny earned." Well, this applies to hundreds of thousands and millions of dollars as well. One hundred thousand dollars saved is one hundred thousand dollars earned. One million dollars saved is one million dollars earned.

The customer is asking you to justify your higher price. The question is basic and simple: "Why should I pay you more?" So now, what are you going to do?

The Wrong Answer

Many sales people will respond by saying, "Our product has quality." They will be trying to use the issue of quality without taking the time to quantify the issue of quality in terms of bottom-line impact for the customer.

I was once working with an organization that sold eyeglass frames to retail opticians in New York City. The managers were complaining about the fierce competition they faced. They told me that when one of their sales people went in to see a customer, there could be two sales people from two competitors completing their presentations. They also told me that when their sales person completed his or her presentation, there could be two sales people from two other competitors coming through the door.

I asked them to explain their sales approach to me.

They told me the sales person would take a box of frames, place it on the counter top, and then discuss the quality of their products.

If this sounds familiar, it should! Most sales people sell this way. They think "quality" is a one-word cure for the price objection.

Take a moment to think about your competition. If you are touting the quality of *your* product, what do you think your competitors are doing? I can assure you that they are not touting the quality of *your* product as well. Rather, they are touting the quality of *their* product.

Unfortunately, if *you* are talking about product quality and *they* are talking about product quality, you have done little to differentiate yourself. You are still left with the $100,000 price differential barrier.

My feeling is that the only way to respond to the price differential question is to quantify the impact of the value ideas contained in your offer, proposal, product, or service. You see, customers will always buy on price until we show them that the price of a product or service is only one element of the total cost of ownership.

Example: The Towering Inferno

My favorite application of this point is contained in the movie, *The Towering Inferno*. The plot of the movie involved a company building a beautiful, new skyscraper. The cost of the construction project was exceeding budget and so the company decided to cut costs in a couple of areas.

One area where it cut costs was in the electrical wiring. The company installed sub-standard wiring in order to help meet the overall project budget.

Unfortunately, the wiring was unable to handle the electrical load and a fire started. The fire became so pervasive that the entire building burned to the ground.

This example is a perfect application of that old saying, "You get what you pay for." Yes the customer received the lowest price on the electrical wiring; however, the total project cost was much higher, since the company had to rebuild the skyscraper.

Lowest Total Cost Solution

All other things being equal, customers may be looking for the lowest price. However, in sales, and in business in general, all other things are never equal.

Customers use price as a decision-making point because it is the easiest way to compare completely different offerings.

However, if your offerings are in fact different (and Chapter 4 should have shown you how to differentiate yourself, your product or service, and your company), then what customers really want is not the lowest price. Rather, they want the *lowest total cost solution*.

The lowest total cost model of selling tells the customer that every decision has implications. For example, if you buy sub-stan-

Supplier	Your Company	Competition
Invoice cost	$100,000	$80,000
Value idea #1	(5,000)	
Value idea #2	(10,000)	
Value idea #3	(15,000)	
True Cost	$70,000	$80,000

Figure 5-2. Which supplier would you prefer?

dard electrical wiring, you may have a fire. Our job, as sales professionals, is to bring out these implications.

In order to raise the visibility of these issues, you must quantify the impact of your recommendations. You must show the customers that your ideas have a tangible bottom-line impact on their business.

Figure 5-2 is designed to present the general challenge that we all face.

If we were to compare these two suppliers on the basis of invoice cost alone, most of us would choose the competition. The basis of our decision would obviously be price.

However, although price is clearly one element of a sales transaction, there are many other elements that need to be considered. Your job is to raise the visibility of the value issues discussed in Chapter 4.

As you can see from Figure 5-2, once the value ideas are factored into the equation, you are really offering the customer a better option. You are offering the customer what I call the lowest total cost solution. You are having a tangible bottom-line impact on the results of the customer's operations. In our example, you are saving the customer $10,000 over the option presented by the competition.

To be successful at value selling, you must become adept at raising the visibility of the value elements of the sales transaction. Again, the best way I know how to do this is to quantify the impact of your recommendations for the customer.

There are four methods you can use to quantify the impact of your ideas:

• Formula

- Assumptions
- Resources
- Norms

Each method is discussed in depth below.

The Formula Method of Value Quantification

The first method of quantifying the impact of your recommendations is the formula method. The key defining characteristic of the formula method is that all of the facts used in your calculation are known.

For example, suppose your customer is performing quality control tests on inbound shipments of your product. Suppose that your company also performs quality control tests on outbound shipments of your product when it leaves your facility.

In this example, let us assume that the customer receives 20 shipments from you every month. You know this information to be true because you can review your shipments to the customer over the last three years.

Let us also assume that it costs the customer $800 per test on inbound shipments. The company knows this to be a fact as well since it recently did a time and motion study on the resources required to perform these tests.

In this example, you could add value for your customer by recognizing that there is a duplication of effort. Your value recommendation could be to run parallel quality control tests for two months. If the results of your tests and the customer's tests are consistent, then the customer can simply rely on your tests. If the customer is unwilling to rely on your tests completely, it can perform sample quality control tests and still reduce the workload.

If the customer elects to fully rely on your tests, the value of your idea to the customer is calculated as follows:

20 shipments per month X $800 per shipment = $16,000 per month or $192,000 per year

The key defining characteristic in the formula method is that all of the facts in your calculation are known. In this case, you were able to obtain the 20 shipments per month from your accounting records. The customer was able to provide you with the cost of performing a quality control test because it had recently performed a time and motion study to determine the cost of performing these tests.

The formula method of quantifying the impact of your ideas simply takes the facts that are known and performs the requisite math. In this case, we took fact A (the number of shipments per month) and multiplied it by fact B (the cost of the quality tests). The answer should be fairly hard to dispute.

Will This Really Work?

If I were delivering a live seminar, someone would raise his or her hand at this point and say, "That's not a great idea. The competition could easily come up with the same idea of dropping or reducing the duplicate quality control tests."

Obviously, competitors could come up with the same idea. And if they couldn't come up with the same idea, they could easily copy your idea once they learned about it.

The purpose of this section of the book is not to develop great ideas. The purpose of this section of the book is to learn how to quantify the great ideas we developed in Chapter 4.

The goal of Chapter 4 was to teach you how to differentiate yourself on the basis of the quality of your ideas. The six ways to add value are the tools that we use to differentiate ourselves. When you take the six ways to add value and you use them in conjunction with the five segments of a customer's business, you have the opportunity to differentiate yourself even further.

At this point, I am assuming that you have great ideas. Our goal is now to learn how to *quantify* them.

Also, I want you to remember Paul's Rule of One—It is never a good idea to approach the customer with just one value idea. The idea that you present may or may not work with that particular customer.

Further, one idea is easy to copy. If you present only one idea, there is a good chance that the competition will copy your idea.

Why not bring a whole bevy of ideas to the customer? This way, if the company rejects one or two or the competition copies one or two, you are still left with a number of ideas through which you can differentiate your offering.

The Assumptions Method of Value Quantification

The second set of questions that participants in my programs always ask me is "Will the customer have access to this information? Will I have access to this information? Will the customer be willing to share its information?"

These are very good questions. The answers to these questions lie in the assumptions method of quantifying value.

The assumptions method is based on the fact that often not all of the information required for the formula method of quantifying value is known. Sometimes the customer does not have access to the information you need. Sometimes you do not have access to the information you need. Sometimes the customer is unwilling to share information on the basis that it may be proprietary.

These are all very common situations, which is why the assumptions method of calculating value has tremendous applicability in the field. In fact, I would venture to say that this may be the most widely used method of the four I am going to present here.

Let me show you how the assumptions method works by way of an example.

Suppose you are supplying your customer with a raw material. And suppose that the company maintains ten days' worth of your product on hand, based on its production needs and your shipping times. Assume that the value of this inventory is $1,000,000.

Assume that you are able to develop a more effective shipping process that will allow the customer to reduce its inventory from a ten-day supply to a five-day supply. (This is your first assumption.)

Also assume that the customer assigns a figure of 10% for the cost of carrying that inventory, because the money tied up in inventory could otherwise be invested and earn the customer a 10% return. (This is your second assumption.)

The value of your recommendation to develop a more effective shipping process can be calculated as shown in Figure 5-3.

There are two tremendous learning points in this example.

First, whenever you develop a recommendation that impacts a customer's inventory, there will typically be two savings: one-time and ongoing.

The first is the cash savings, a one-time, first-year increase in the customer's cash position.

Original inventory balance	$1,000,000
New inventory balance	500,000
Cash savings to customer	500,000
Inventory carrying costs	10%
Inventory carrying savings to customer	50,000

Figure 5-3. Illustration of the assumptions method of quantifying value

As you know, cash may be a company's most precious commodity. Cash allows the investments that can grow the business. Companies do not want their cash tied up in accounts receivable and inventory. Anything you do to help your customer reduce either accounts receivable or inventory levels gives the customer an advantage.

In this example, we are reducing the customer's inventory levels from $1,000,000 to $500,000. This results in a one-time conversion of $500,000 from inventory to cash. In other words, you have just put $500,000 of cash into your customer's pocket.

But the savings do not stop with this one-time savings. The second savings is ongoing. You are also saving the customer $50,000 per year in inventory carrying costs. (Remember that the company assigns a cost of 10% to money held in inventory.) And that savings in inventory carrying costs continues from year to year.

(Although our example is with inventory, a similar analysis would apply if your recommendation had an impact on the customer's accounts receivable level.)

How to Build Barriers to Keep Out Competitors

All of us would love to keep the competition out of our accounts. The example in the prior section shows us how to do this.

Many of the value ideas that you implement are cumulative: the benefits continue from year to year.

Imagine that you are working with an account that is buying $100,000 worth of your service per year. This is your first year in working with the account and you are able to develop value recommendations that save the customer $10,000.

Assume that these value recommendations are cumulative, just like the inventory carrying cost reduction example above. This means that at the start of year two, you will still be bringing the $10,000 worth of value to your customer. This also means that the true cost of your service is no longer $100,000; it is now only $90,000.

Assume that in year two you develop a second $10,000 in cumulative benefits. Now, the true cost of your service is only $80,000, not the $100,000 that appears on your invoice.

Now let us jump to the fifth year of your relationship with the customer. Each year you've continued to bring the company $10,000 in cumulative value. This means that the true cost of your service is now only $50,000. This also means that any competitors must charge less than $50,000 in order for the customer to switch to them on the basis of price.

As sales professionals, we all want to build strong relationships with our customers. Many sales professionals interpret relationship building as taking a customer's representative to a ball game or playing a round of golf with him or her.

This is a good way to build a relationship, but I believe it is the second step in the process. The first step in the process is to build the relationship by making it financially unfeasable for the customer to leave. You do this by continuing to add value to the company's sales cycle. Once you have made the customer successful in this manner, then take the representatives to the ball game to enhance the quality of your relationship.

Some Final Thoughts on Assumptions

As you can see, the assumptions method is based on the fact that not all of the factors in your formula may be known. In the prior example, we made two assumptions. The first assumption related to the reduced shipping times and the second assumption related to the inventory carrying costs.

Assumptions are made in business all of the time. When a company decides to open a new factory, the decision-makers are basing their plans for the future success of the factory and the business on assumptions. When a company decides to purchase another company, the decision-makers are also basing their plans for the future success of the company and the business on assumptions. When you purchase a stock in the stock market, you are also basing your decisions on assumptions. You are hoping that the price of the stock will rise.

Assumptions permeate every aspect of business and it is certainly valid to let them enter into sales. After all, when someone purchases a product or service from you, he or she is making assumptions that the transaction will improve his or her business operation.

How to Make Assumptions

In order to use the assumptions method of quantifying value, you must become adept at making assumptions. The key to making assumptions is to *involve the customer* in each step of the process.

In fact, customer involvement is the key to every method of value quantification discussed in this chapter. The customer must believe in the data, whether the data is based on assumptions or facts, in order for the value quantification process to work.

If the customer does not believe in the data, the value quantification will not work. This is true even if you could prove to a third party that the data you are using is correct. If your customer does not believe in the data as correct, you will have very little success in getting the customer to support and accept your quantifications.

I thought it would be useful to show how the assumptions process works, so I've constructed a sample conversation with a customer based on the prior example.

Let us assume that you are trying to determine the value your customer assigns to inventory carrying costs. Here's how the conversation might develop:

You: What value do you assign to inventory carrying costs at your company?

Customer: Gee, that's a good question. We had a meeting about this just the other day and were unable to develop an answer.

You: As you know, I work with a lot of companies, both within your industry and outside of your industry. 10% seems to be a good number for inventory carrying costs for most of my customers.

It's important that you develop more than just product expertise. To succeed at the type of selling that I am advocating, you must have overall business savvy. You must understand that accounts receivable and inventory are two of the customer's largest assets. You must also have a general understanding of inventory carrying costs, return on investment, and other general business and financial measurement tools.

Remember that our goal in this book is to differentiate ourselves based on the quality of our ideas. Our goal is also to make our customers more successful as a result of these ideas. Our ultimate goal is to derive our success as sales professionals from the success of our customers.

In order to reach these goals, we must go beyond the obvious. We must do things a little differently from the other sales people who call on your customer. We must become adept at creating and delivering value to our customers.

Unfortunately, product knowledge alone is insufficient to do this. You must be prepared to move from sales person to business consultant. Only business consultants will be successful at delivering value to their customers. And to be a business consultant, you must have some expertise in the operations of your customer's business as a whole.

OK. You have now placed an assumption in front of your customer. You have just said that a value of 10% works for many of your other customers. At this point, the customer can only say one of three things—that the value of your assumption is too high, too low, or right on target. Let's take a look at how all three situations play out.

(value too high)
Customer: I don't know. 10% percent seems high to me.
You: Tell me what you believe a better value to be.
Customer: How about 8%?
You: That sounds fair to me.

(value too low)
Customer: I don't know. 10% percent seems low to me.
You: Tell me what you believe a better value to be.
Customer: How about 12%?
You: That sounds fair to me.

(value OK)
Customer: 10% seems fair. Why don't we use that figure?
You: OK.

You see, when working with a customer to develop an assumption, all you need is a starting point. A good starting point should be based on information you have gained from working with other companies, both within the customer's industry and outside the customer's industry.

Knowledge, as we discussed in a prior chapter, is the most powerful tool for the sales professional. Start to become knowledge-conscious. Start to gather information that would be valuable to both your customers and your prospects.

Once you place a starting point on the table, the customer has only one of three choices. As we illustrated above, your assumption may seem too high, too low, or right on target. If the customer says your assumption is too high or too low, ask for a more appropriate value. Of course, if your assumption seems on target, accept it and move on.

It is a fairly simple matter to work with your customer to arrive at an assumption that both you and the customer can support. As you begin to implement this process in the field, keep in mind that it is more important for your customer to support the assumption than it is for you to support the assumption. Any assumption with a value greater than zero is good for you.

In the prior example, even if the customer assigned only a 1% value to inventory carrying costs, we would have still achieved our goal. After all, 1% of $1,000,000 is $10,000, which is still significant. If you couple this $10,000 with Paul's Rule of One, you will see why you have achieved your goal.

Paul's Rule of One states that you should never bring just one value idea to the customer. Rather, you should bring many. So even if the customer lowers all of your assumptions, the value of the diminished assumptions will still be significant.

If you have five value recommendations, each with diminished values of $10,000, you have brought $50,000 of value to your customer. And this is in just one year. You may have also delivered $50,000 in value to the customer in the prior year and you have the opportunity to deliver unlimited value to the customer next year.

The key to making assumptions is to get customer support for the assumptions.

What if the Customer Doesn't Want to Share?

There is actually a fourth outcome to the scenario developed above: the customer may not be willing to share information to develop a good assumption. Then what do you do?

The answer to this question is easy. Give your customer the model with your own assumptions.

One of our major accounts in my computer training business was the United Nations. We had been the exclusive provider of computer training for the UN for a period of five years.

The United Nations was required to put its contracts out for bid every five years to ensure that it was getting a good deal in the market. Our contract had come due and was put out to bid.

There were 21 companies just like ours in the market and every one of them received the United Nations' request for proposal. One of those companies was from the West Coast and it was trying to expand into the New York marketplace.

Apparently, this new competitor had significant excess capacity and entered a very low bid just to get some business. Its bid, as we later found out, was 50% lower than the lowest bid from the remaining companies.

Needless to say, the UN was attracted to that offer and selected the company as its new vendor of choice.

Our account manager was quite upset. A major portion of his income was derived from sales to the United Nations.

He called up his customer of five years to ask for a meeting. He and the UN contact had grown very close over the duration of their relationship. He was sure he would get a second chance.

Not only had our account manager developed a close relationship, but also our performance during the five years had been superlative.

The United Nations had required that we deliver training to UN personnel in all of the world's "hot spots." We had delivered training in Addis Ababa, Ethiopia. We had delivered training in Lebanon. We had delivered training in Croatia. There were actually instances where our trainers had been under fire as they went to and from their classes—and it had nothing to do with the quality of the program!

We never missed a beat. Every program we delivered met with rave reviews.

So our account manager called for a meeting, but his request was denied. He couldn't believe it.

He came to me and asked for advice.

All I could think of was quantification.

After all, the customer had left us on the basis of price. Why not try to show that the price of a product or service is only one element of the total cost of the relationship?

We went through every idea we could in terms of creating value. We quantified each and every one.

We thought about what values we could deliver over the next five years and quantified these as well.

When we were through, we had quantified such significant value that we could clearly prove that the UN would be better off with us in spite of the competitor's lower price.

We called for another meeting. After all, we had new and powerful information to present.

Our request was denied again. The contract was now in the UN legal department.

As a last resort, we decided to fax our quantifications to the customer. I felt as though we were on a desert island sending a message for help in a bottle we found on the beach.

The contact received the quantifications and looked them over. The decision makers must have entered their own assumptions, because they called us in to review the models we had provided. The meeting went well and they pulled their contract out of the legal department and awarded it to us.

Customers may not always share information with you so that you can use the assumptions method of quantifying value. When customers play their hand a little close to the vest, I would encourage you to develop your models on your own. Enter in your own assumptions and leave it for the customer to review. Here's how this scenario might play out:

You: I was wondering what value you assign to inventory carrying costs at your company.

Customer: Well, we consider this to be proprietary information.

You: I can understand that. However, I have developed a model that you may want to take a look at. Why don't I leave it behind in case you find it of value?

When the customer will not provide you with the information you require to develop your assumptions, at least leave the model so that you can begin to get the company thinking about your value quantification.

Status quo is the bane of the sales professional. If the customer does nothing different from the prior year, you will find it very difficult to further penetrate your current accounts and very difficult to win new ones.

The name of the game in professional sales is to get your customers to evaluate new information. When customers are evaluating new information, the opportunity for change exists—and that's what we want as sales professionals.

Oh, by the way, if you are still thinking about the UN story I just told, you should be. Yes, it was like pulling a rabbit out of a hat. I told you this story because there are times when you will be operating under less than optimal conditions. There will be times when the customer is unwilling to share information with you.

However, great sales people are strategic thinkers. Great sales people never quit. Great sales people are always developing new and innovative ways to approach their customers. And this example illustrates the power of giving your customers the models, even in the absence of customer-specific data with which to make them work.

Yes, the account manager should have been delivering this information to the customer throughout the five-year relationship. Yes, the account manager should not have left the quantifications to the last minute. However, that was the situation we were in and the models were able to carry us to success.

Chapter 6 is going to show you how the UN account manager should have been operating throughout the five-year period. We are going to present you with an approach to integrate everything we have discussed in the book thus far into your day-to-day selling activities.

But now, let's take a look at the next method of quantification.

The Resources Method of Value Quantification

The resources method of quantifying value is used any time you include a resource as part of your overall product or service offering.

A resource would be any element of time, tools, people, or capital that comes with your product or service.

One classic application of the resource method would be when you include extended credit terms as part of your product or service package.

For example, suppose that it is customary in your business to have 30-day credit terms. This means that your customers are supposed to pay your invoices within 30 days of the invoice date.

Suppose that, instead of the customary 30 days, you offer your customer 60-day credit terms. Here, you would be offering them a resource—capital. If you did not offer the customer the extended credit terms, the company would have to go to a bank and borrow money for a period of 30 days in order to pay your invoice.

Suppose that the customer in question has an average outstanding accounts receivable balance with your company of $100,000. This means that, were it not for your offer, the company would have to go to a bank to get a credit facility of $100,000. Assuming that the current interest rate is 8%, the value of your recommendation would be $8,000.

The defining characteristics of the resource method are twofold.

First, you are including an element of time, tools, people, or capital as part of your overall product or service offering.

Second, the resource you are providing can typically be purchased in the open market. Because the resource can be purchased in the open market, there is a readily established market price for the value you are delivering. It is this market price that must be used in your calculation.

A second classic example of the resources method is when you provide a technical resource to the customer to help it overcome day-to-day operating challenges.

Assuming that you provide the resource for 10 hours per month, and similar technical resources can be purchased on the open market for $100 per hour, the value of your recommendation is $1,000 per month or $12,000 per year.

Many Resources Have an Assumption of Equal or Greater Value

It is important for you to understand that many resource calculations have a second element of value that must be considered.

In the second example above, we included 10 hours of technical service as part of our product or service offering. We then calculated the value of the 10 hours of technical service based on market prices.

However, we did not consider the impact of the technical service provided.

Suppose that you are providing raw materials to a manufacturing concern. Earlier in this book, we talked about factory downtime as being a critical success factor in a manufacturing environment. We assigned a value of $20,000 per hour to factory downtime, based on our knowledge of our customers and the industries within which they operate.

Many factories run 24 hours per day, seven days per week. Let us assume that your technical service representative is able to improve productivity for your customer by 1%. The value of this recommendation, using the assumptions method, would be calculated as seen in Figure 5-4.

How Much Can I Really Save the Customer?

Figure 5-4 illustrates two key points.

First, for many resource calculations, there is an assumption of equal or greater value. The question you must ask is "Does the resource have an impact on the customer organization?"

Second, the cumulative value of your recommendations may be significant. In this example, we were able to save the customer in excess of $1,700,000.

When you become adept at creating, delivering, and quantifying value, it should not be at all uncommon for you to deliver value to

Days in year	365
Hours in day	24
Hours in year	8,760
Productivity improvement	1%
Improvement in hours	87.6
Savings per hour	$20,000
Dollar savings	$1,752,000

Figure 5-4. Calculation of an assumption of equal or greater value

the customer in excess of the amount of your annual billings to the customer. In other words, when you add up all of your invoices to the customer and deduct the value you delivered, the result is either zero or a negative number.

What Does This Mean to Me?

Because you have the opportunity to deliver value in such tremendous quantities, you clearly have the opportunity to charge price premiums in the market.

In fact, if you return to Figure 5-2, you can see that you are charging a 25% premium over the competition. Yet your $100,000 invoice cost is actually a better deal than the competition's $80,000 invoice cost, because the true cost of your product or service is only $70,000.

However, our opportunity does not end here.

If you compare the true cost of your offer ($70,000) and the true cost of the competitive offer ($80,000), you would see that you still have $10,000 of value to share. You could in fact raise the price of your product by $10,000 before the customer would have a valid business reason to switch back to the competitive offer.

The Norms Method of Value Quantification

Norms is the final method of quantifying value. You use the norms method whenever you make a process improvement for the customer.

In an earlier chapter we talked about process improvements. There we noted that process improvements come in two forms.

First, you can help a customer complete a process faster. For example, if your customer is producing five widgets per hour, your process improvement may help the company increase production to six widgets per hour.

Second, you can help a customer complete a process more efficiently. For example, if your customer is producing six defects per day, a process improvement may reduce the defects to five per day.

The norms method is used to measure the process improvement.

Figure 5-5 illustrates the use of the norms method.

We start by calculating the impact of the process improvement. In this example, we can improve the customer's process by one unit per hour. The hourly improvement is then converted to a daily improvement, since the customer runs production 24 hours a day. We then take the unit improvement and convert it to a dollar improvement, since our goal is always to have a tangible bottom-line impact on the results of operations of our customers.

Hourly widget production in units	5
Hourly widget production with process improvement	6
Process improvement in units	1
Manufacturing hours per day	24
Process improvement per day	24
Gross margin on one unit	$1,000
Dollar process improvement per day	$24,000
Dollar process improvement per year	$8,760,000

Figure 5-5. Illustration of norms method

It is important to note that our conversion formula uses the customer's gross margin for the product, not its selling price. In order to be accurate in our calculations and maintain our credibility with the customer, it is important that we consider the cost of product development as well as its related revenue.

Finally, we convert the daily process improvement to an annual process improvement, since this is the basis upon which the customer will measure us.

Conclusion

The goal of this chapter was to show you how to illustrate that your recommendations have a tangible bottom-line impact on the results of your customers. In order to do this, you must quantify the impact of your recommendations.

The bottom line in business is success. To excel in today's business environment, you must be able to demonstrate success. I think you will agree that this is exactly what we have done in this chapter.

The next chapter is going to show you how to integrate the ideas in this book into your daily selling opportunities.

Chapter 6

The Value Audit

This book is devoted to making your customers red-hot. This book is also devoted to making your sales career red-hot by deriving your success from the success of your customers.

However, in order to make your customers red-hot and make your sales career red-hot, we must learn how to integrate the ideas we have presented in this book into our day-to-day selling activities.

This is the purpose of your value audit.

A Case Study of Success

In an earlier chapter, I told you about a sales person who worked for me who was able to make one of her customers more successful by making it easy to do business with our company. Her ideas were a great source of value to the customer. Now I would like to tell you the rest of the story.

The account in question was an institution in the marketplace, one of those "must have" accounts. Unfortunately, this account had a long and successful relationship with one of our competitors. The company was quite happy with its current provider *and* getting a great price.

It seems as if there was no way to wrest the account from the competition.

In fact, the competition was so deeply entrenched with the account that we felt we were only making an obligatory sales call each quarter to pay our respects to this great company.

The last time we visited the prospect, it was a cold, rainy day in New York City. If you have never been in New York City on such a day, you wouldn't know about the wind tunnels created by some of the large buildings. The wind was whipping into our faces and the rain was driving through our coats. We were freezing!

But we had to pay our respects.

We got to the company and were about to take off our coats when the contact told us that we didn't have to make ourselves comfortable. We had effectively paid our respects and that was good enough. He would see us next quarter when the time came to pay homage again.

If I seem a little facetious in telling this story, it is by intention. I am just trying to emphasize how desperate our position was with this account.

I was resigned to our position and getting ready to brave the cold winter day again, when the account manager said, "I didn't come here to sell you anything. We came to perform a *value audit*."

The contact was intrigued by her comment and wanted to learn about the value audit.

She explained that she just wanted to ask the contact a few questions to see if the company was using its computer training services provider in an optimal manner. If she concluded that that was the case, she would write the customer a letter to that effect. But if there were room for improvement, she would write the customer a report—at no charge—telling about the ideas she'd developed.

She even went so far as to tell the contact that, if the company felt the ideas in the report had merit, it could implement them with us or even with its current provider.

On the other hand, if the company did not like her ideas, it could dispose of our report without obligation.

The contact asked our account manager to continue.

What Is a Value Audit?

A value audit is the tool that we use to properly position ourselves for success with the customer.

A value audit is the tool that we use to penetrate accounts with which we are currently not doing business.

A value audit is also the tool that we use to build barriers to entry for the competition.

Finally, a value audit is a series of questions that we use to identify value-selling opportunities for the customer or prospect.

In fact, the quality of your value audit will be directly related to the quality of the questions that you ask. And since questions are crucial to your success, I think it would be a good idea to review the types of questions you can ask in a value audit of your customer.

Your Value Audit Questions

There are three types of questions that you can ask in a value audit—value-discovery questions, value-refinement questions, and value-leading questions.

Value-Discovery Questions

Value-discovery questions are the heart of the value audit process. Value-discovery questions are questions that require a detailed response from the customer. Value-discovery questions are similar to open-ended questions in that they are used for probing or gathering customer information.

However, in addition to probing or gathering customer information, value-discovery questions are specifically designed to allow you to discover value-selling opportunities.

Value-discovery questions can help you identify the niche selling opportunities that we discussed in Chapter 5. It is your value-discovery questions that will allow you to either penetrate an account or build barriers to entry.

Value-Refinement Questions

Value-refinement questions are questions that are used to test the information gathered in the value-discovery process. Value-refinement questions are similar to closed-ended questions in that they can typically be answered with brief statements.

For example, suppose that you have uncovered a value-selling opportunity with one of your customers. The opportunity arose as a result of your value-discovery process.

Suppose that you were proposing an idea that would integrate your order entry system with the customer's purchase order process. A question such as "Do you believe that an idea like this would work in your business?" would be a good value-refinement question.

Here, your value-discovery process uncovered a need: the need to reduce the time it took the customer to process an order with a company like yours. You then proposed to integrate your system with that of the customer.

Before you begin to take this idea further, it would be a good idea to test the validity of your idea. After all, the customer may consider the idea to be a good one, but the company may be unwilling to implement the idea for one reason or another.

Value-refinement questions can test whether it would be worth your time and effort to pursue this idea further. The question "Do you believe that an idea like this would work in your business?" allows you to test the idea.

Value-Leading Questions

Value-leading questions are the third category of questions that are typically used in a value audit. Value-leading questions come in most handy when working with customers to emphasize the value points in your proposal.

Value-leading questions are designed to get the customer to think.

As you know, sales professionals are usually better off when we can get the customer to think. If your contact is thinking, he or she is less likely to accept the status quo. If you have an account relationship, the customer will be more likely to let you further develop that relationship. If you are trying to penetrate the account, the prospect will be more likely to make a change.

Value-leading questions can be either open-ended or closed-ended. While there is no general way to phrase a value-leading question, the following would all be good examples of value-leading questions:

- Have you considered the impact of reduced downtime on the results of your operations?

- Would an improvement in your safety record be important to you?
- What would be the impact of reduced shipping time on your operations?
- Would improving your customer service rating be important to you?

In each case, the customer is asked to consider a new set of facts or circumstances. The value of leading questions is that they get the customer to consider new evidence in its decision-making processes.

A Sample Value Audit

Let's return to our story of the account manager who was able to use a value audit to wrest a major account from the competition. I would like to show you just how she did it.

The product we were selling was computer training.

We were visiting a major account that had been working with one of our largest competitors for years. The prospect was happy with the level of service the company was receiving and, *most important*, the prospect felt the company was receiving a great price.

Your Value-Background Question

The first question that our account manager asked in her value audit is what I call a value-background question. Your value-background question is a value-discovery question and serves to update your understanding of the account.

If you have been working with or have visited this account, this is a good question to ask since the situation may have changed since your last contact. If you have not worked with this account, this is a good question since it will allow you to begin the information-gathering process with this prospect.

Our account manager asked, "What are you doing now in the area of computer training?"

This is a great question to get your value audit off the ground and can be used in almost any business or industry.

For example, if you were selling plastics, you might ask the customer how the company handles its plastics purchases now. And if you were an Internet service provider, you might ask the customer how the company currently uses the Internet.

This question is useful to gather information about annual

usage, current pricing, sources of purchase, and more. You can also use it to make certain that you are dealing with current information in your understanding of the account.

Our account manager was able to use this value-background question to find out the customer's current source of supply, pricing structure, and mode of delivery. Her goal with this question was to establish a baseline understanding of the customer's business practice as it related to the products we were selling.

Your Value-Penetration Questions

Now that you have an understanding of the customer baseline as it relates to your product or service, you must look for ways to either penetrate the account (if this is a target prospect) or expand your account relationship (if this is a current customer).

The next two questions in your value audit are intended to show you how to either penetrate new accounts or build barriers to entry with current accounts. We call these questions value-penetration questions, since they allow you to start or expand account relationships.

After our account manager had updated her baseline understanding of the prospect, she asked the first of her two value-penetration questions.

Our account manager asked, "Given what you are doing now in computer training, are there areas for improvement?"

She struck gold with this question.

What she learned was that the prospect had an extensive waiting list for computer training classes. She also knew about a study just released in our industry that explained that the cost of purchasing a computer was only about 25% of the total cost of ownership. The remaining 75% related to ineffective technology usage.

Our account manager was quickly able to determine that the extensive waiting list was costing the customer over $600,000 annually due to ineffective technology usage.

One recommendation that she would make in reporting the results of her value audit would be to reduce the length of its training programs by optimizing the skills taught in the programs. This would then reduce the length of the waiting list and improve technology usage. The impact of this one recommendation alone would save the customer $600,000 annually.

Back to Our Core/Niche Strategy

Before we move on to the next question in the value audit, let's take a moment to review what we have accomplished thus far.

With one question, we were able to uncover an opportunity to save the customer $600,000 annually. If you were to compare this with the customer's annual computer training expenses of about $200,000, you can see why we were so excited about the opportunity.

The customer could be paying $200,000 for computer training and receiving $600,000 in return. This means that the "true cost" of its computer training services, if the company purchased from us, would be a negative $400,000. What this meant to us is that we had quite a bit of flexibility in terms of pricing our product.

Remember that the customer felt the company was receiving a good product and a good price from the competition. A value idea such as the one outlined above clearly gives the customer a strong financial incentive to switch to us. In fact, we could have charged the customer up to $800,000 per year because of this one idea alone before we would have put ourselves in a comparable position with the competition.

When you review this question, you should see that we are trying to execute the core/niche account penetration strategy that we introduced in Chapter 5. The core/niche strategy tells us that the best account penetration strategy over the long run, the strategy that will yield consistently good results, is the strategy that helps you seek out and benefit from niche selling opportunities. The essence of a niche selling opportunity is to deliver something to the customer that it needs but does not have.

Back to Value Penetration

We have now completed the second question in our value audit and the first of our two value-penetration questions.

The first question we asked in the value audit was: *What are you doing now in the area of computer training?*

We asked this question to establish a baseline for the remainder of our value audit.

The second question we asked was: *Given what you are doing now, are there areas for improvement?*

We use the third question in our value audit to continue to develop our core/niche strategy. This question is also designed to either position us for our first sale or expand an account relationship.

Our account manager asked, "Can you tell me about your future direction?"

This question can uncover customer needs that are not yet being met. This is quite easy to do with future needs, because future business is always up for grabs. Therefore, future business is by definition a niche selling opportunity.

Unfortunately, with this account this question did not uncover an opportunity that we could capitalize on. However, the goal of our value-penetration questions is quite clear.

The purpose of our value-penetration questions is to uncover a business opportunity, a chance to provide something that the customer needs but does not have. This could come in two forms.

First, we could help the customer improve upon its current position. Second, we could help the customer realize future goals and objectives. In either instance we would be delivering something that the customer needs but does not have. We are executing our core/niche strategy and we are beginning to differentiate ourselves in a competitive market.

Why Does the Core/Niche Strategy Work So Well?

The core/niche strategy is such a powerful account development tool because it capitalizes on the natural progression of account evolution.

Large account relationships typically develop according to a development cycle. I do not mean to imply that large accounts will never materialize early in the sales cycle. We all know that they will. However, this is the exception and not the rule.

Most large account relationships develop over time. This means that we must have a well-developed account strategy in order both to penetrate and to develop the account relationship. To help you develop your account strategy, I have developed what I call the account development cycle.

The Account Development Cycle

The account development cycle tells us that most account relationships develop according to a very predictable pattern. If we can understand the account development cycle and related pattern, we will be able to improve upon our account penetration strategy. We will be able to increase our chances of success in the sales cycle.

The account development cycle consists of the following pattern:

- Identify your customer's needs.
- Position your company in relation to those needs.
- Make your first small (niche) sale.
- Make your second small sale.
- Make a larger sale.
- Position yourself for exclusive provider status.
- Expand your account penetration.
- Proactively manage the account.

Assuming that you are working with a prospect account, one that you have never done business with, the first step in the account development cycle is to identify the customer's needs. This is the purpose of the value audit.

(Please don't worry that we are starting with a prospect and not a customer. We will consider current customers when we move further into the account development cycle.)

Once we have identified the prospective customer's needs, we must start to position our company for success, for a sale. This leads us to the second step in the development cycle, to position your company in relation to the customer's needs.

I firmly believe that you should complete the value-discovery process prior to starting to position your company with the customer. The tendency of many sales people is to ask a question and then try to make a sale.

Although you definitely want to make a sale, you will be more successful to the extent that you can further differentiate yourself from the competition. The only way you can do this is to gather as much information as possible before you start to show the customer how you can help.

Remember that Paul's Rule of One tells us that if we can help the customer in only one way, we may not have done enough to position ourselves for success. However, if we can help the customer in many ways, we will have gone much further down the differentiation curve.

After you have positioned your company in relation to the customer's needs, the next step in the account development cycle is to try to make your first small sale. Your first small sale is the niche selling opportunities that we have discussed both in this chapter and in Chapter 5.

By asking the customer about "areas for improvement," you are trying both to identify a niche selling opportunity and to make your first small sale. By asking the customer about the company's "future direction," you are also trying to identify a niche selling opportunity and to make your first small sale.

Making small sales is a crucial point in the account development process. Again, I do not want to imply that you should not try to make large sales. You clearly should. However, typically a larger sales opportunity will not present itself until we have moved further into the development cycle.

Remember that the single largest impediment to a sale is the question, "Will it work?" Typically, a prospect will not be willing to test your company on a large business opportunity because there is too much risk. A smaller business opportunity or a small sale is the best way to test a new provider.

Further, the larger business opportunities tend to be more closely related to the core. The core business for your customer is that portion of its business for which solutions are readily available in the open market. Because the opportunity has many direct alternatives, you will generally find yourself selling on the basis of price.

Small sales are the best way to penetrate accounts over the long run. Small sales are the niche selling opportunities that we have been stressing. Small sales are also the value-selling opportunities upon which this book is based. Small sales, niche sales, and value sales all bring customers something they need and do not have. Small sales, niche sales, and value sales all position you for success with customers. Small sales, niche sales, and value sales will also typically command premium pricing in the market because of the few directly comparable alternatives.

Once you have made your first small sale with an account, you want to start to think about gaining your second and third small sales. Small sales are the best way to develop a track record with an account. Small sales are the best way to answer the question, "Will it work?"

When I was in the computer training business, one of my largest accounts was Merck. We were Merck's exclusive provider for computer training during the seven years that it was the most admired company in the world.

However, our relationship with Merck did not start out large. Rather, it started out very small, with our first small sale. We had called Merck on the phone (yes, cold calling still works!) and were able to set up a face-to-face selling appointment.

When we arrived at Merck, we learned that the company was re-evaluating its current provider and was soon going to issue a major request for proposal. We told Merck that we wouldn't even respond to the request for proposal because we felt we had no chance of winning. We had never done even one dollar of business with Merck and felt that the track records of some of our competitors would be too extensive to allow us win the business by simply writing a great proposal.

We argued very strenuously for Merck to give us the opportunity to make one small sale to the company. Finally, we won. The company agreed to allow us to deliver one computer training class so that we could begin to establish a track record.

We delivered the program and it went well. We were now in a position to respond to the request for proposal, but we felt that we had to build a much better track record with Merck if we were to have any chance of winning. And so we began to search for our next small sale.

We learned that Merck was a beta test site for Microsoft products. This meant that when Microsoft was developing a new version of a software application, Merck would receive a pre-release copy of the software for both use and testing at the company. We also learned that Microsoft was willing to pay companies like ours to deliver training on the pre-release software. After all, if we could show companies like Merck how to more effectively use the application, Microsoft would be more likely to make future sales of the product.

We were able to arrange for Microsoft to pay us to deliver several additional computer training classes at Merck. This was our second small sale and a great example of niche selling.

Remember that a niche sale is one that is not readily available in the open market. Here, the software application was not yet released and we were ready to deliver the training. We were able to do so because of a special relationship we had developed with Microsoft that allowed us to receive pre-release copies of the software before they went out to the corporate market.

I would also like to point out that this was one of our company's unique selling points. We prided ourselves on being "consistently first to market" with new training products so that companies could minimize their ineffective use of the new technology applications.

I point this out because it is crucial to understand that the unique selling point concept that I presented in Chapter 2 is directly related to the value audit concept that I am presenting here. In fact, the value audit is the summary of every idea I have presented thus far.

Every strategy and tool in this book is focused on one goal, to *effectively manage customer perceptions about what is important in a relationship*.

Managing customer perceptions is crucial to your success.

If you review the steps of the purchasing process, you will see that it is the customer's perceptions that allow you to move from one step in the sales cycle to the next.

If there are 10 potential vendors in the market, a buyer will not survey all 10 with equal intensity. Rather, a buyer will quickly survey the 10 and decide which two or three vendors warrant further consideration. The buyer makes this preliminary market assessment based on its perception of which vendors will best serve its needs.

Then, the buyer will make a more extensive review of the two or three finalists to determine which one company best suits its needs. Finally, the buyer will decide on the basis of its perception of which vendor can make it the most successful.

Your job as a sales professional is to manage customer perceptions. Everything that you do as a sales professional you should do with one goal in mind—to make customers "think properly." If we can make customers believe what we believe, they will always select us. If they believe differently, they will choose the competition. It's as simple as that.

When you make a cold call, you should be trying to manage customer perceptions. It is for this reason that I am happy both when I speak with a customer on the phone and when I get voice mail from a customer. In either instance I have the same ability to manage perceptions about what is important in a relationship.

Why It Is Good for the Customer to Work with a Single Provider

Many companies believe that they are better off playing one vendor off against another. This is a strategy that companies typically use to get vendors to lower their price.

A customer will tell vendor B that vendor A has offered a lower price. Vendor B will then have to meet or beat the price in order to earn the business.

However, when vendor B meets or beats the price, the customer turns back to vendor A. It is now vendor A's turn to beat the last bid.

Customers feel that they get the best deal this way and also keep vendors from becoming complacent.

Believe it or not, it is actually in the customer's best interest to have one primary provider of a product or service. This is not to say that the customer should not have a backup in case the primary supplier cannot meet its requirements. This is also not to imply that a customer should not survey the field to make certain it is receiving a quality product at a good price.

Customers should feel free to keep their options open. However, customers should also consider the evidence available to them and make the best financial decision for their companies.

The first major benefit to the customers comes in the form of economies of scale. Companies will typically benefit from longer production runs in the form of cost reductions.

If the customer takes its business and divides it among many suppliers, there is not enough business for any one provider to benefit from longer production runs. Therefore, the cost of providing the product or service is maintained at an artificially high level. This is true even though the customer will likely play one provider against another to get the best price.

The customer would be better off in most instances by making a major commitment to one provider, letting that provider mold its production schedule to the customer's needs, and passing on to the customer cost savings from economies of scale in production.

Besides saving on longer production runs, the customer can also reduce costs by integrating its systems with those of the provider. Multiple suppliers mean multiple invoices to process and multiple systems to learn. This means added time and cost to the customer.

In addition to the cost savings through economies of scale and integrating systems, the customer may also benefit from working more closely with a supplier in terms of new product development or future expansion plans.

When we responded to the Merck request for proposal, we were able to demonstrate that the benefits of exclusive provider status outweighed the risks. Merck selected us as its exclusive provider. We were now providing the company with solutions for both its core needs and its niche needs.

Can You Rest on Your Laurels?

At this point, you might think we were at the pinnacle of selling success. After all, we were the exclusive provider to Merck and Merck was the most admired company in the world for seven years running.

It clearly does not get much better than this.

Unfortunately, you cannot rest on your laurels as a sales professional. As soon as you begin to become complacent, one of your competitors can begin to use the core/niche strategy against you.

Remember that the core/niche strategy was what let us penetrate the account in the first place. This is the best account penetration strategy I have come across. However, if it will work for you, it will also work for your competitors.

When you become the exclusive provider, you must continue to execute the core/niche strategy. If you are not going to identify the next niche opportunity, your competition will. Therefore, whether you are trying to penetrate an account or to build barriers to entry, you must continue to seek out new niche business with your customers.

This is why the questions from our value audit that ask about "areas for improvement" and "future direction" are so powerful. They apply to any situation in which you are trying to make your customer more successful. This is true whether you are new to an account trying to make your first sale or you are the exclusive provider trying to build barriers to entry.

This is also why we have put an additional step in the account development cycle.

Many sales people believe that exclusive provider status is the pinnacle of account management. While this is a great position to occupy, you must constantly strive to expand your relationship with the customer. If you are not trying to locate and execute the next niche opportunity, a competitor most certainly is.

The Pinnacle of Account Management

The true pinnacle of account management is not exclusive provider status. The true pinnacle of account management is what I call *proactive account management*. Proactive account management occurs when your value strategies have been so successful over the long run that the customer outsources its decision-making process for your product or service to you.

As you will see in the next chapter, our company reached this level with Merck.

If you think it is difficult to attain this level of relationship with an account, you are correct. This level of relationship can be developed only through exceptional performance over the long run.

If you have ever worked with a stockbroker who has done a great job for you, you may have reached proactive account management with him or her. Many investors have stockbrokers who manage their stock portfolios. After many years of exceptional performance, you may have outsourced your investment management decision making to your stockbroker. If so, he or she is proactively managing your account.

Take it from me: proactive account management is the top of the sales world.

Your Value-Management Question

We have now asked three questions in our value audit.

The first was the *value-background* question: *What are you doing now in the computer training area?*

We asked this question establish our baseline with the account.

The second and third questions were our *value-penetration* questions: *Given what you are doing now, are there areas for improvement?* and *What is your future direction?*

We asked these questions in order to execute the core/niche account penetration strategy.

The fourth question our account manager asked was: *What is important to you in a relationship with a company like ours?*

Remember, sales is the successful management of customer perceptions about what is important in a relationship. The first step in managing customer perceptions is to understand exactly what those perceptions are. This is the goal of your *value-management* question.

This question will tell you whether the customer values a low price, reliable delivery, product or service quality, or any of the other variables that can impact a sale.

Your objective at this point in the questioning process would be to determine if the customer's value system aligns with your strengths as an organization. In effect, you would like to build a bridge between the customer's needs and your unique selling points. If you can succeed in this bridge-building process, you will likely make the sale. If you cannot succeed, your competitors will have a greater chance of making the sale.

In a perfect world, the customer's values will always align with your unique selling points and you will make every sale effortlessly. However, this is not a perfect world and we will usually have to work very hard to make certain that the customer's value system is in alignment with our strengths.

In fact, this is exactly what happened in our value audit. Our account manager asked the customer what the company considered important in a relationship with a company like ours. The customer responded that in order to displace the competition we would have to offer a really great price.

Remember that the competition had been working with the customer for some time now. The customer felt that it was receiving a great product at a great price.

The Value of Leading Questions

When customer values are not in alignment with your strengths, you must use leading questions to facilitate the process through which the customer considers new evidence.

Notice how tactfully I just phrased it: "facilitate the process through which the customer considers new evidence."

Whenever you are working with customers, please consider that they have typically made substantial investments in their value-development process. And once anyone has made substantial investments of time and/or resources in any thought process, it is very difficult to challenge his or her decisions and be successful at either changing that person's mind or building a relationship.

Consider any perception or thought you have. You may have spent many years of your life developing that thought or perception. This is why it is so difficult to change. You have a large investment in your current mode of thinking.

Also, consider a typical selling situation where the customer wants a lower price. A sample discussion along these lines might proceed as follows:

Sales Person: Do I understand you correctly when you say that price is the most important variable in your decision-making process?

Customer: Yes, you do. Things are tougher around here than they have been in the past and management has asked all of us to tighten our belts. Lowering our supplier pricing is the best way I know of to tighten our belts.

Sales Person: Are you sure that lowering supplier cost is the best alternative? I used to think lowering supplier cost was a good idea too. However, you get what you pay for. We all know that.

Customer: We feel pretty comfortable in our approach to vendor management. It's something we've thought a lot about and all of our purchasing managers are moving in the same direction.

Sales Person: I hear where you're coming from, but I still think you need to consider additional options. Sure, my price is higher than the competition; but we all know that our quality is superior.

Customer: Your quality may very well be superior. I have no way of knowing that. For our application, though, most of the vendors out there have quality that is good enough.

Sales Person: I agree that the competition has quality products. However, their products do not have our new technology.

As you can see, this type of conversation could go on forever. It has been my experience that the longer this conversation proceeds, the more obstinate the customer tends to become.

A better alternative is to ask leading questions so that the customer can consider new evidence and draw his or her own conclusions as to what is right or wrong for the company. A conversation taking this latter tack might proceed a little differently, as illustrated below:

Sales Person: I understand that things are tough and that, like most companies, you are trying to tighten your belts.

Customer: You've hit the nail on the head. We're trying to economize.

Sales Person: What's the single largest cost you face in your production process?

Customer: Oh, that's easy. The single largest cost factor we face in our production process is downtime. downtime costs us approximately $20,000 per hour.

Sales Person: If I could introduce a process improvement that would reduce downtime in your factory by one-tenth of 1%, would that have a major impact on your bottom line? (This is your value-leading question.)

Customer: Major! It would save us millions. It would change the way we do business. I would love to be the person who presents this idea to the boss.

Sales Person: Great! Let me tell you about the process improvement and see if we can draw up the agreements today.

Customer: Sounds great to me.

The differences in approach between the first sales person and the second sales person are subtle yet powerful.

In the first instance, the sales person tried to convince the customer that she is wrong. While customers may very well be wrong, pointing this out to them is rarely your path to success. Rather, they will likely feel even stronger about their position because you have challenged it.

On the other hand, the second approach allowed the customer to draw her own conclusions. As you can see, giving customers the opportunity to consider new evidence and draw their own conclusions can generate very powerful results.

Remember that sales is *the successful management of customer perceptions about what is important in a relationship.* The use of value-leading questions is one of the best ways to get customers to consider new evidence.

The Last Question in Your Value Audit

We have now asked the customer four questions.

The first question was intended to establish or update our background information. The second and third questions were intended to enable us to implement our core/niche strategy. The fourth question was intended to allow us to understand and manage customer perceptions.

The final question in your value audit is to make certain that you have uncovered every possible element of value. You might conclude your value audit by asking the following question:

Is there anything else I need to know (or you would like to tell me) in order to make our relationship as successful as possible?

This question gives the customer one last opportunity to tell us about a need that the company may have that we have not uncovered with the line of questioning outlined above.

Your Value Audit Worksheet

Your value audit worksheet is presented in Figure 6-2. Your value audit worksheet is a tool that is designed to embody all that we have discussed in this chapter.

As you can see from Figure 6-2, the first portion of your value audit worksheet is your *objective*. Here, we are asking you to set an objective for your value audit. What are you hoping to accomplish by going to visit the customer?

My assumption is that you are trying to advance the sale or move further into the account development cycle. That is why we have provided you with the account development cycle on your value audit worksheet.

What we are asking you to do is to determine where you are in the sales cycle. Once you have determined where you are, you need to set an objective. We recommend that you consider moving to the next step in the sales cycle.

For example, if you are currently at the small sale stage, you might set as your objective to move to the larger sale stage of the development cycle.

The next section of your value audit worksheet is your *strategy*.

This section of the worksheet is designed to get you to start thinking about differentiating yourself in a competitive market.

You may be familiar with the story about a purchasing agent who has a large fish mounted on his wall. A sales person walks into the purchasing agent's office, greets the agent, and then delivers a compliment about the beautiful fish: "That's a mighty fine fish you

| **Your objective** | Introduce your company
Identify the prospect's needs
Gain a small sale
Gain a larger sale
Obtain exclusive providership
Expand account penetration
Proactively manage account evolution |

Your strategy

| **Your agenda**
What are you doing now in the area of...? | Your USP I
Your USP II
Your USP III
Your USP IV
Your USP V |

Are there any areas for improvement?

What is your future direction?

What's important to you in a relationship?

Is there anything else I should know?

Your next step:

Figure 6-2. Value audit worksheet (USP = Unique Selling Point)

have on the wall. You must be very proud and a great fisherman as well."

The purchasing agent responds rather smugly, "I don't fish at all. I just put the fish there to see how many sales people would make note of it in an effort to gain my favor."

Prior to your value audit, select one of your unique selling points to be the lead point of your meeting. This is not to imply that your other unique selling points will not work with this account. They may. This is also not to imply that other information gained during the value audit may not be useful to you. It most certainly will. However, you want to have a game plan going into the audit.

Suppose, for example, that one of your unique selling points is that you are a global organization. You have offices throughout the world, while many of your competitors are smaller, regional players.

The big advantages for the customer are that it could receive the benefit of your global distribution system, it could receive more timely deliveries of your product, it could access your local support system, and it could receive more timely response on all support calls. In addition, it would receive only one invoice per month for your worldwide services, in contrast with receiving numerous invoices from different suppliers.

Based on your knowledge of the customer and your prior dealings with the customer, you feel that your global capabilities would be the one point that, above all others, would help you close the sale. This would be the starting point for your strategy.

Now that you have a strategy in place, you have two ways to present this idea.

You could simply tout the benefits of your global capabilities. This is what most sales people would do and it is exactly what the customer would expect.

A better approach would be to have someone else tout the benefits of your global distribution system. You may be thinking about using references from other customers at this point, but that is not what I have in mind. References would typically come into play later, when you need to either overcome an objection about your capabilities or help the customer overcome buyer's remorse.

What I had in mind is to reach out to business journals like *The Wall Street Journal*, *USA Today*, and local business publications or trade publications to look for evidence about global capabilities being a great selling point and a strong customer benefit.

For example, there could have been a recent article in *The Wall Street Journal* about how XYZ Company better served ABC Company because of its worldwide locations. Once you have an article that supports your strategy, the strategy section of your value audit might proceed along these lines.

You: Mr. Jones, it's great to see you. How are you today?

Mr. Jones: Fine. How are you?

You: I'm great, thanks. Say, did you see the recent article in *The Wall Street Journal* about XYZ Company?

Mr. Jones: No. Why do you ask?

You: Well, I thought it was really interesting how XYZ Company was able to save ABC company over $1,000,000 because of XYZ's global distribution system. I brought you a copy of the article.

At this point, you have accomplished three things.

First, you have begun to differentiate your company in the marketplace. You are no longer competing with the other sales people who come into Mr. Jones' office to talk about the fish on the wall.

Second, you have begun to position yourself as a consultant. I believe that one of the most important tools we have as sales professionals is information. In fact, information, or business know-how, was one of the sources of value that we developed in Chapter 4. By sharing information like this with Mr. Jones, you are both providing value and positioning yourself as a consultant.

The third and most important goal you have accomplished here is that you have started to execute your strategy for the value audit. You have worked with the customer in the past and you know that a global distribution system is critical to its success. Your company has one of the best distribution systems in the marketplace and you feel that this capability is critical to your success in the sale.

What you have done by introducing *The Wall Street Journal* article is to lend third-party credibility to your argument or position. Please note that you would not make your argument with Mr. Jones now, but rather when you present your solutions.

Remember: customers expect us to tout the benefits of our distribution system and so they discount any positive remarks we make in this regard. What is difficult to discount, however, is evidence from a credible third-party source, such as *The Wall Street Journal*, that is making the exact same point.

Customer perceptions are crucial to your success.

There is one additional interesting point that must be made here. We are dealing not with reality but with perceptions.

Take the example we have developed above. It is not necessary for us to have the very best global distribution system in the marketplace in order to use this idea as either a strategy or a unique selling point. Rather, it is only important to have a very good distribution system.

The point that is crucial to understand is that your unique selling points are a matter of perception. Ownership of a unique selling point goes to the company that is considered to be first in the category, not the company that actually is first.

Selling is the effective management of customer perceptions about what is important in a relationship. Your job as a sales professional is to raise the visibility of your unique selling points in the market so that you can be perceived as first in your unique selling point category.

Back to Your Value Audit Worksheet

The third section of your value audit worksheet is your *agenda*. Here is where you use your five value audit questions.

Your five value audit questions are designed to help you understand each customer's needs. This should be the focal point of your value audit. However, while you are looking for customer needs, you should also be looking for customer needs that you can serve. Most important, you should be looking for customer needs that you are uniquely qualified to serve. This is why you have included your unique selling points in your value audit worksheet as well.

I always think of building a bridge between my unique selling points and the customer's needs. I feel that if I can be effective in the bridge-building process, I have a sale. If I cannot be effective, I obviously have more work to do.

The final section of the value audit worksheet asks you to plan your next step with this particular account.

The purpose of your value audit worksheet is to give you a process through which you can manage and deliver your value audits. Believe it or not, I still use the value audit worksheet on every face-to-face sales call that I make.

Conclusion

This chapter gave us a process through which we can implement our value-selling strategies with the customer. The next chapter of the book will deliver what I call "the ultimate selling tool"! I'm not going to tell you what it is here. You'll have to read the next chapter to find out.

Chapter 7

The Ultimate Selling Tool

When we developed the concept of the value audit in Chapter 6, we learned that sales is the *successful management of customer perceptions about what is important in a relationship*. If you view sales in this manner, you will see that the art of successful sales is actually quite simple, because there will be only three variables involved in a sale:

- the customer's needs
- your offering
- the offering of the competition

You should know by now when I refer to either your offering or the offering of the competition, I am referring to your *total* offering. Your *total* offering is not just your product or service, but rather, your entire relationship with the customer. This includes both the product or service and all of the layered value that you add to the product or service.

Chapter 6 also showed us how a sale is made and why most sales will typically conclude with these three elements.

If you recall, when there are ten providers in a market for a particular product or service, the customer will typically make a preliminary survey of the companies to find those organizations that are

136

serious contenders for the sale. This survey is made based on the customer's perceptions of the offer each organization brings to market.

Often, this survey is made without direct contact with a sales professional. In other words, the customer is making its preliminary assessment of your product or service prior to ever meeting with you.

Because customers may make their preliminary assessment of your organization prior to working with you, it is critical that you become adept at managing customer perceptions before your first face-to-face meeting with the customer.

In Chapter 2, we talked about how to deliver your red-hot cause to market. There, we defined your company's five unique selling points and gave you a multitude of tools that you could use to raise the visibility of your unique selling points and red-hot cause.

We even told you the story of a man trying to break a rock with a sledgehammer. We noted that his success would be based on the cumulative efforts of his blows, not on the basis of any one strike. This story also taught us that there was a parallel between your selling success and the man's success in breaking the rock.

In sales, your prospects are your rock, your unique selling points are your hammer, and the tools outlined in Chapter 2 (your newsletter, your press releases, your public speeches, and others) are the blows you deliver to the rock. These tools allow you to bring your message to market, to manage customer perceptions prior to your first meeting, and ultimately to break your rock.

The value of these tools becomes very clear at this point.

Customers often survey the market prior to their first contact with you. Customers make their preliminary survey on the basis of who they believe will best suit their needs. If we are not adept at bringing our message to market, we could lose many sales before we even enter the battle.

In order to enter the battle, we must become adept at managing customer perceptions prior to making our first face-to-face contact with the customer. This is why we spent the time to show you how to bring your red-hot cause to market.

Once you have been selected as one of the two or three finalists in the customer's purchase process, the customer will begin a detailed evaluation of your offer and the offers of the other finalists.

A review of the purchasing process will reveal what I consider to be the essence of selling success.

The Purchasing Process

Here are the four steps in the purchasing process:

1. Determine the current buying criterion.
2. Influence the final buying criterion.
3. Differentiate your offering.
4. Create a perceived fit with the buying criterion vis-à-vis the competition.

The first step in the purchasing process is to determine the current buying criterion.

Because customers have spent time surveying the market prior to their first contact with you, and because customers have likely thought about the application of your type of product or service in their business, they will have an idea of what they are looking for in a company like yours.

If you refer back to the questions we asked in our value audit, you will see that the fourth question—"What's important to you in a relationship with a company like ours?"—was designed to help you understand the customer's current buying criterion.

Determining the customer's current buying criterion is the first step in the purchasing process.

I do not believe that you can be effective at selling if you do not know the customer's current buying criterion. If you do not know what the customer values in a relationship, you will have little opportunity to work with the customer's perceptions so that you can be successful in the sales process.

It is interesting to note that most, if not all, customers have a current buying criterion. That is, they have a perception of what is important to them before we enter the sale. Finding out what is important to the customer is the starting point for your sales effort.

The second step is to influence the final buying criterion.

Just because our customers have developed a perception of their needs prior to our meetings does not mean that we have to accept those perceptions hook, line, and sinker.

For example, suppose that you are working with a customer and ask, "What's important to you in a relationship with a company like ours?" Suppose the customer says price is the most important vendor selection criterion. I hope that at this point in the book you will not say, "OK, let me see what I can do to get you a better deal."

Much of selling takes place at this step in the purchasing process. Customers have perceptions prior to entering the sales cycle. Our job as sales professionals is to manage those perceptions so that the customers get the best solution for their needs.

Here are the strategies that I have come across that will allow you to manage customer perceptions:

1. Introduce new criteria into the sales process.
2. Expand the scope of the existing criteria.
3. Provide combinations of existing criteria.
4. Quantify the impact of your recommendations.
5. Improve on the existing criteria.
6. Provide the customer with valid alternatives.

To the extent that you can succeed in implementing these strategies, you will be more successful in the sales cycle. To the extent that you cannot succeed in implementing these strategies, the competition will be more likely to win the sale.

How to Manage Customer Perceptions

The first way to manage customer perceptions is to *introduce new criteria into the sales process*. This involves developing new criteria for the purchase decision instead of using the ones supplied by the customer at the start of the sale.

For example, earlier in this book we told you about one of my customers who is a domestic manufacturer of large factory equipment. The price of this company's equipment is often 40% higher than the price of the foreign competition.

Many of its customers use price as their default purchasing criterion. However, this comany has been successful at pointing out that service is more important than price in the purchase of equipment.

They have been able to do this by helping their customers understand that the largest cost in a purchase of this nature is not the price of the equipment, but rather the cost of downtime when the equipment doesn't work. They estimated that the cost of one hour of downtime for their customers was approximately $20,000. My client guaranteed next-day parts and service for repairs. The foreign competition could guarantee only next-week parts and service.

They were able to demonstrate that one breakdown per year would more than offset the price differential and were successful at making their customers understand that service was perhaps a better purchase criterion than price in this instance.

They were successful at introducing a new purchase criterion into the customers' sales process. They were also successful at managing customer perceptions about what is important in a relationship.

A second way to mold customer perceptions is to *expand the scope of the existing criteria.*

As you already know, another of my customers is in the environmental services business. A typical application for this company's service is to clean oil tanks. I went on a sales call with one of the company's account managers. The customer wanted the account manager to bid on a tank cleaning application. Tank cleaning is considered to be a commodity service and the customer was heavily focused on price.

The account manager could have simply offered his best price because this is exactly what the customer wanted. However, the account manager insisted on taking a walk through the job site and determined that the customer had neglected to include waste removal in the original project specification.

By expanding the customer's selection criteria, the account manager was able to differentiate his company from the competition and win the sale.

A third way to manage customer perceptions is to *provide combinations of current criteria.* Here, you can use combinations of current and new criteria to help construct a new set of selection criteria for the customer. This approach often borders on sales negotiations and can be illustrated in a very simple way.

Suppose your client is heavily focused on price and your price tends to be higher than that of the competition. You can offer something in addition to your product or service to offset the perceived price differential. In this instance, you could offer an extended warranty, free training and installation, extended payment terms, or absorb the shipping costs, as opposed to charging them to the customer.

The point I am trying to make is that when you cannot bend or bend significantly on a given issue, you still have the option to add additional variables to the sale to develop new purchase criteria for the customer.

There are two great learning points here.

First, recognize that you will often be placed in a position to negotiate a purchase or offer tradeoffs to a customer or prospect. I have found that listing all negotiating or tradeoff variables prior to meeting with the customer will greatly enhance your chances for success in the negotiations process.

I have compiled a list of common tradeoff variables below:

- Price
- Payment terms
- Delivery
- Warranty
- Training
- Installation
- Length of agreement
- Volume of agreement
- Pre-payments
- Financing terms
- Customer support
- Other variables particular to your industry

My recommendation is to take the list above and customize it to your business. The more variables you can develop, the better your negotiating position.

After you have developed your list, prioritize the variables in order of importance to your company. This way, when you have to be flexible on one issue, you can get something back of value to your organization on another issue.

When I was in the computer training business, I noticed that many of our customers were negotiating on the basis of price. In other words, they wanted a lower price than the one we offered.

Our account managers were adept at asking in return for items valuable to our business. For example, the most popular response when the customer asked for a lower price was to ask for a contract pre-payment. Yes, I said *contract pre-payment*.

As a growing business, cash was always a valuable commodity to us. However, many of our customers were *Fortune* 2000 companies with ample supplies of cash in relation to our contract price. We found that many of our customers were quite willing to pay for a year's worth of services in advance in return for a price concession. We, of course, used the pre-payment to offset the price reduction that we negotiated with the customer.

If you cannot get your customers to pre-pay for your products or services, there are still many items left on the list above. You could ask for a longer contract term (two years as opposed to one, for example), lower pricing in year one and higher pricing in years two and three, increased contract volume, or premium pricing on niche products or services.

There are an endless number of possibilities here—which brings us to our second great learning point on this topic. The second great learning point is that any time there is only one variable in a sale, the sales person usually loses. Earlier in the book, we called this "Paul's Rule of One."

Again, assume that your customer wants a lower price and price is the only remaining variable in the sale. If we give the customer a lower price, we obviously lose on this sale. However, if we do not give the customer a lower price, we still lose on this sale.

The reason we lose in the second instance is because we have probably damaged the relationship. The customer will be looking for ways to extract price concessions in subsequent sales transactions.

The fourth way to manage customer perceptions is to quantify the impact of your recommendations to the customer. The methods of quantification were discussed in depth in Chapter 5 of this book.

As we illustrated there, this is a very powerful selling tool. At this point, I would only like to remind you about the impact of quantification by sharing with you one of my favorite sales quotes. The quotation is taken from John Ruskin, a 19th century English social theorist, and is entitled "Low Bid":

It is unwise to pay too much, but it's worse to pay too little. When you pay too much, you lose a little money.... That is all.

When you pay too little, you sometimes lose everything because the thing you bought was incapable of doing the thing it was bought to do.

The common law of business balance prohibits paying a little and getting a lot.... It can't be done. If you deal with the lowest bidder, it is well to add something for the risk you run, and if you do that you will have enough to pay for something better.

The Ultimate Selling Tool

Referring back to the strategies to change customer perceptions on page 139, there are still two additional methods of helping the customer best understand what's important to them in a relationship.

The first of these two additional methods is *helping the customer better define or improve upon the current criteria.*

This is my favorite method, since it is the one I have had the most success with. We developed our approach here quite by accident; however, it turned out to be the single most powerful and broad-reaching sales idea that I have ever used.

Earlier in this book, I told you the story of how we were able to win the Merck account when that company was the most admired in the world, seven years running.

Well, our first contract with Merck expired and Merck wanted to place our contract out to bid in order to be sure of getting the very best products and services available in the market.

By Merck's own account of the relationship, we were doing a great job. However, the company still wanted to test the market.

Keep in mind that Merck was the most admired company in the world at this time and having the Merck account was a great feather in our cap. There were 21 other companies in the market just like ours and Merck was going to send out a request for proposal to all 22 companies.

We were quite concerned about this and asked the representatives from Merck how they were going to draft their request for proposal to make certain that they selected the best possible partner for their needs.

They hadn't really thought about this question and asked us to draft their request for proposal.

At first, we were unhappy about the additional work that we had to do and felt that Merck was taking advantage of us. However, we got to work and drafted the request for proposal.

Before we put our pens to the paper, we began to do a little strategizing. We wondered if there was anything we could do with the request for proposal to increase our chances of success in the proposal process.

We decided to draft the Merck request for proposal around our unique selling points.

We knew that we couldn't be obvious about what we were doing, since Merck was well aware of our unique selling points. After all, we had spent a great deal of effort positioning our unique selling points in the marketplace. If we were obvious, the Merck representatives would know what we were up to and this would diminish the credibility of our efforts and of our request for proposal.

What we did was to develop a request for proposal around a generic version of our unique selling points.

For example, one of the areas we were particularly proud of was the overall strength of our organization. In terms of our unique selling points, this took the form of our national delivery system (most of our competitors could only deliver locally), a broad portfolio of products and services, and a strong administrative backbone.

When we developed the request for proposal, one of the areas we selected for detailed questioning was the overall quality of the organization writing the proposal. A second area we tested for was the depth of the organization's administrative systems.

The great learning point here is that we felt we could control the customer's decision-making process if we could incorporate our unique selling points into the proposal process. Effectively, we were helping the customer decide what was important to it in a relationship with a company like ours.

We developed the Merck request for proposal and believed that the strategy of incorporating our unique selling points into the proposal process would help manage the customer's perceptions about what's important in a relationship. We felt that we were starting to stack the deck in our favor.

However, keep in mind that we were working with Merck, the most admired company in the world. We knew that all of our competitors would give the new Merck request for proposal their very best shot. While we felt that we had a strong competitive advantage by being the incumbent provider, we were not secure in our position.

We felt that being the author of the request for proposal would certainly strengthen our position; however, we could not afford to lose this account.

It wasn't the Merck business volume that was the most important part of the relationship. Rather it was the Merck aura and the credibility it gave to us as an organization.

Over the two and one-half years that we had done business with Merck, we learned that the credibility of the Merck reference was unparalleled. I couldn't begin to count the number of sales we made as a result of being Merck's exclusive provider. It was almost as if all we had to do on a sale was mention to the prospect that the idea we were proposing to them was one that we had already implemented at Merck. There was a general market perception that "if it's good enough for Merck, it's good enough for my company."

We didn't want to lose this one and were unsure if writing the request for proposal would guarantee us the sale. So we asked the Merck representatives the next question.

We asked them how they were going to evaluate the proposals they received. After all, there were 21 companies just like us in the market and we knew they would all try to win the proposal process by weight. We felt that each company would send in a 100-page proposal. We wanted to understand how Merck was going to evaluate the 2,100 pages of information it would receive in order to select a vendor.

What we learned was that Merck had ten people on its vendor selection committee and they didn't have a well-defined vendor selection process in place. We believed that this only compounded the challenge Merck faced. After all, each of the committee members would now have to evaluate 2,100 pages of information to make a good vendor selection.

Merck wasn't sure how they were going to do this and asked us to develop a vendor evaluation matrix.

The vendor evaluation matrix we developed for Merck is presented in Figure 7-1 (pages 146-147).

The Merck vendor evaluation matrix was designed to work hand in hand with the proposal we had developed. The purpose of the matrix was to ensure that the customer followed the evaluation procedure that we felt best suited our needs.

Remember that sales is the successful management of customer

XYZ Company Training Partner Analysis					
Weighting	**Area/Category/Criterion**	**Vendor 1 Ratings (1-20; 10 = Avg)**	**Vendor 1 Weighted Score**	**Vendor 2 Ratings (1-20; 10 = Avg)**	**Vendor 2 Weighted Score**
25%	**Vendor Overview**				
11%	**Background**	7	8%	10	11%
	Stability (years in business, ownership, size, finances, executive management)				
	Distribution network (geographic match, control–owned/franchise/affiliate)				
	Business partners (software, publishers, third-party relationships)				
	Training philosophy				
	Account management team (talent, stability, track record, flexibility)				
	Extended services (outsourcing, technical writing, materials development, Learning Centers/TDI, courseware licensing, technique training, consulting)				
	Quality assurance procedures				
3%	**Facilities**	12	4%	10	3%
	Proximity to XYZ Company				
	Capacity				
	Hardware capabilities				
	Legal software				
	Duplicate XYZ environment				
	Appearance				
11%	**References**	4	4%	10	11%
	XYZ				
	Outside references				
40%	**Instructor-Led Training**				
10%	**Courses**	6	6%	10	10%
	Breadth of offerings				
	Technical offerings				
	Responsiveness to new products				
	Flexibility to customize courses and materials				
	Soundness of instructional design				
	Student and instructor materials review				
15%	**Customization**	5	8%	10	15%
	Modularity				
	Customization methodology				
	Documentation of customization methodology				
	Example of customization				
	Depth and quality of development resources				
	Ability to develop new XYZ-specific materials				
	Ability to work with XYZ departments				

Figure 7-1. Vendor evaluation matrix (continued on next page)

Weighting	Area/Category/Criterion	Vendor 1 Ratings (1-20; 10 = Avg)	Vendor 1 Weighted Score	Vendor 2 Ratings (1-20; 10 = Avg)	Vendor 2 Weighted Score
15%	**Instructors**	12	18%	10	15%
	Staff expertise				
	Certification process/quality control				
	Backup procedures				
	Understanding of XYZ culture				
	Continuing education programs				
	Résumés				
	Size of staff				
	XYZ instructor team				
15%	**Technology-Delivered Instruction**				
9%	**Learning Center**	7	6%	10	9%
	Design and development expertise				
	Knowledge of TDI products				
	Understanding of ILT/TDI/JITL integration				
	Examples				
	Relationship with TDI suppliers				
5%	**Counseling**	10	5%	10	5%
	Training program/certification for counselors				
	Support resources for counselors				
	Background and expertise of counselors				
	XYZ Learning Center team				
	Backup procedures				
1%	**Development**	15	2%	10	1%
	Development capabilities				
	Examples				
20%	**Administrative Services**				
7%	**Registration**	10	7%	10	7%
	Registration system capabilities				
	Administrative team				
	Remote access by XYZ including e-mail				
	Flexibility to customize service to XYZ				
	Registration tools (screening, etc.)				
7%	**Measurement**	7	5%	10	7%
	Methodology				
	Examples				
	Measurement tools				
	Flexibility to customize to XYZ				
6%	**Reporting**	5	5%	10	6%
	Capabilities				
	Flexibility to customize to XYZ				
	Integration with registration system				
	Analytical ability of acct. mgt. team				
			77%		100%

Figure 7-1. Vendor evaluation matrix (continued)

perceptions about what is important in a relationship. I believe that to the extent you can manage customer perceptions, you will be more likely to win the sale. To the extent you are unsuccessful in this process, your competition will have a strong advantage in this transaction.

Merck accepted our request for proposal and vendor evaluation matrix with some modification and we won the new Merck contract.

However, I believe that the Merck account was ours to lose. After all, we were the incumbent on the Merck account. We should have won the new contract on the basis of our relationship with Merck alone.

Because we were the incumbent on the Merck account and because the account was ours to lose, I didn't understand the sales value of the tools that we had just created. We had just created the ultimate selling tool, but were too close to the Merck account to understand the power of what we had just accomplished.

We didn't understand the power of the matrix until several months later. We had arranged for a sales call at Allied Signal, another great company in our market.

Like Merck, Allied Signal was evaluating its current provider. Allied Signal had been using the same company, one of our competitors, for years and the company was quite happy with the relationship. However, like Merck, Allied Signal wanted to test the market to make certain that its relationship was as beneficial as it could be.

We had never done business with Allied Signal, but started to ask the same questions we asked of Merck:

How are you going to develop your request for proposal?

How are you going to evaluate the proposals you receive?

What we learned was that Allied Signal had just formed a vendor selection committee and we were talking to the chair. Further, the person we were talking to was responsible for developing both a request for proposal and a vendor evaluation matrix.

We asked if our contact would be interested in reviewing some work that we had done for another client. We wound up giving our Merck request for proposal and vendor evaluation matrix to our contact at Allied Signal. The only change we made to the documents was to change the names from Merck to Allied Signal.

We were not present when our contact presented his findings to the committee. However, rumor has it that he presented both the proposal and evaluation matrix as his own, without modification.

In other words, Allied Signal had adopted our decision-making process. We also won the Allied Signal account.

We won the Allied Signal account before making our first small sale at Allied Signal. This is quite profound when you consider the account development cycle that we presented earlier in this book.

The account development cycle taught us that most relationships start small. Therefore, when you are trying to penetrate an account for the first time, you need to look for your first small sale.

The account development cycle also told us that the risk for the customer to move from introduction to exclusive provider in one step is too high. Rather, customers would mitigate their risk in a new relationship with smaller sales.

In spite of the wisdom found in the account development cycle, we were now Allied Signal's exclusive provider.

This experience taught us about the power of the ultimate selling tool. The matrix was designed to manage customer perceptions about what is important in a relationship. Allied Signal adopted our decision-making process without modification. Therefore, we fully managed its perceptions in this sales process and won the sale.

We learned that to the extent that you can manage customer perceptions about what is important in a relationship, you will always win the sale. To the extent that you are not successful in the value-management process, the competition will be more likely to win the sale.

Once we knew this, our goal became to devote all of our energies to the customer value-management process. Our goal became to insert our matrix into every major account selling situation we encountered.

When we were successful at inserting the matrix into the customer's decision-making process, we always won the sale. When we were not successful at inserting the matrix into the customer's decision-making process, we won only our fair share of sales.

To the extent that you can be successful at managing the customer's decision-making process, you will win the sale. The purpose of the matrix, the ultimate selling tool, was to help us manage customer perceptions about what's important in a relationship.

How to Develop Your Own Vendor Evaluation Matrix

At this point, you should be wondering if you could develop a matrix for your business. The answer is, of course, yes! We are going to give you the process for developing a matrix that you can use in your business.

As you begin to develop your ultimate selling tool, please consider the following points.

First, you will have to make a significant investment of time in developing your ultimate selling tool. We did—and we did not enjoy the process the first time through. We felt that Merck was taking advantage of our relationship by asking us to develop the matrix.

Once you have a matrix in place, however, you can use the matrix time and time again with different customers and prospects. The matrix is most useful in major account selling situations. We were successful at using the matrix with companies like Merck, Allied Signal, American Express, Citibank, and Prudential Insurance, to name a few.

Allow your customers the option to modify the matrix and the request for proposal. This lends additional credibility to the process. We always presented the matrix and request for proposal to our customers on disk. We found this increased customer support for the process and also found that customers rarely, if ever, modified what we gave them.

Step 1 in developing your vendor evaluation matrix is to develop the major categories to the matrix. We recommend that you develop four or five major categories for your matrix. Each major category should be designed to capture and quantify the customer's perceptions of a supplier's performance relative to each of your five unique selling points. Remember: make each category generic so that the customer will not be able to draw an immediate association between the categories in the matrix and the unique selling points you position in the marketplace.

Step 2 is to have the customer develop relative weightings for each category. The relative weightings are designed to measure each category's importance in relation to the customer's decision-making process. In other words, the customer could give category one 25% importance in its total decision-making process, category two 5% and so on. The assessments or ratings must total 100%.

Note: When we were developing our quantifications in Chapter 5, we told you that customer support for your assumptions was of paramount importance to the process. If the customer did not support your assumptions, this would severely impair your ability to develop quantifications that would justify your premium pricing in the market.

Your ultimate selling tool is no different. You must have customer support for the matrix or its validity as a vendor evaluation tool will be limited. Make certain that the customer supports your four or five major categories.

One great way to gain support is to allow the customer to fully develop the weightings discussed above. By allowing the company representatives to develop the weightings, you allow them to feel they have a strong part in the vendor selection process.

The battle that we need to fight here is not over the *weightings* but rather over the *categories*. The categories in the matrix are designed to mirror your unique selling points. Once you establish categories in this manner, the importance of the weightings is greatly diminished. After all, the customer is simply rating your strengths relative to one another.

Step 3 in the process is to develop two or three minor categories for each major category presented. The reason for minor categories is so the customer fully understands the definitions you intended for the major categories. For example, Figure 7-1 shows Vendor Overview as the first major category. In our example, it received a 25% rating in terms of relative importance to the customer. The minor categories relating to Vendor Overview are Background, Facilities, and References. Have the customer rate the minor categories in terms of relative importance to the major category. Here, Background received a minor relative weighting of 11%, Facilities a minor rating of 3%, and References a minor rating of 11%. The minor ratings must total the major rating of 25% for this category. Note that the minor categories are also designed to help you get buy-in from the customer. Here's where you can mold the major category definitions so that the customer will support your overall position.

Step 4 is to develop descriptive text for each minor category. Descriptive text for each minor category is also used to define the customer's interpretation of both the major and minor categories discussed above. Descriptive text is also a great tool to gain customer buy-in if you allow the customer to participate in the development of the descriptive text. Figure 7-1 shows, for example, that the minor category Background was described using the words Stability, Distribution Network, Business Partners, and so on.

Step 5 in the process is to further define each element of descriptive text so as to avoid any potential confusion in the evaluation stage of the proposal process. If you think we are going to great lengths to manage customer perceptions about what is important in a relationship, you are correct. The reason we are doing this is because much of the selection process in a major account sale like the ones I have been describing takes place when the sales professional is not with the customer. Customers will review product literature, proposals, presentations, and other material we provide without us present. It is for this reason that we must be extremely particular in the perception-management process. You can see in Figure 7-1 that the descriptive text Stability was further defined as years in business, ownership, size, finances, and executive management. The sub-description process is also designed to get buy-in on the part of the customer.

Note: Neither the descriptive text nor the sub-descriptions enter into the evaluation process. They are both included in the matrix to avoid ambiguity and to gain customer buy-in.

Step 6 in the process is probably the most crucial. Thus far, we have asked you to develop both a request for proposal and a vendor evaluation matrix. It is of paramount importance that the request for proposal and the vendor evaluation matrix work together. In other words, if you were to return to Figure 7-1, you would find the first major category in your vendor evaluation matrix is Vendor Overview. This must also be the first major category in your request for proposal. The first minor category in your vendor evaluation matrix must also be the first minor category in your request for proposal. In Figure 7-1, we used Background as our first minor category. Finally, the descriptive text in your matrix should also follow the same order as the information gathered in your request for proposal. This will provide for a one-to-one correspondence between the request for proposal and the vendor evaluation matrix.

It is important to note that only you will know there is a one-to-one correspondence between the request for proposal and the vendor evaluation matrix. None of your competitors will. Therefore, you will have a competitive advantage in the proposal development process. I would recommend as step 7 that you also develop a proposal to work with the request for proposal and vendor evaluation matrix. This way there will be a one-to-one correspondence among all three documents. The beauty of this strategy will become apparent in the next step.

Step 8 is to have the client assign a numeric value to each vendor in each minor category. For example, Figure 7-1 shows a numeric score of 7 in the Background area for Vendor 1. Vendor 2 is given a numeric rating of 10 in the same category. Please note that we used a scale of 0 to 20 for rating each vendor. The reason we used a wider scale than, say, 1 to 5 or 0 to 10 is to allow for sufficient differentiation among vendors. Please also note that a score of 10 is considered to be "average" for a vendor in your marketplace. This means that if your organization received a score of 12 in a given area, you would be considered above average in this area relative to the other companies in your marketplace. A score of 8, on the other hand, would mean that you are below average relative to the other companies in your market.

Note: In step 8 of this process, we said that having a one-to-one correspondence among the request for proposal, the vendor evaluation matrix, and the proposal would yield a strong competitive advantage. Now, we are in a position to explain why.

Your competitors will receive the request for proposal. They will not receive the vendor evaluation matrix. Therefore, when they prepare their proposal, they will not understand the value of preparing their proposal with the same headings and sub-headings that appear in the matrix. Further, they will not see the value in preparing the proposal and matrix in exactly the same order. This will make their proposal more difficult to rate than yours.

For example, the customer may not be able to find the sub-heading Customization in the competitive proposal. This appears in section 2, under Instructor-Led Training, in Figure 7-1. The customer has assigned a weighting of 15% to this element of your business. If the customer is unable to find this section on the competitive proposal, the competitor would be assigned a score of 0 for 15% of the proposal.

Step 9 in the process is to develop the relative importance scores for each vendor in the marketplace. You can develop the relative importance score by taking the relative importance assigned to each category in step 2 above and multiplying it by the absolute score you received in the prior step. With reference to Figure 7-1, you can do this by taking the rating found in column 1 of the chart and multiplying it by the score received in the vendor columns of the matrix. Let's use Vendor 1 as an example. You can develop the relative importance score for that vendor in the Background category by taking the relative importance score found in column 1 of the matrix (11%) and multiplying it by the score of 7 in the Background area to obtain a relative importance score of 7.7%. This has been rounded off to 8% in Figure 7-1.

The final step in the process is to total the relative importance scores for each vendor. The vendor with the highest relative importance score wins. Therein lies the great application of this tool. If you recall, the ultimate selling tool was built around your unique selling points or the strengths of your organization. It should naturally lead the customer, therefore, to picking you above the competition.

The request for proposal, the matrix, and the proposal are all designed with one goal in mind. The purpose of these tools is to allow us to control the process through which the customer makes the decision.

In a normal selling situation, one often has little control over the customer decision-making process. This is why we are tempted to revert back to price as a factor to differentiate our company and gain favor with the customer.

By controlling the customer's decision-making process, or what I call the "playing field," you stack the deck in your favor in any competitive bidding process. The extent to which you can control the playing field determines the extent to which you are likely to win the sale. If you have strong control over the playing field, you will likely win the sale. If you have only limited control over the playing field, your chances of success are much smaller.

The Playing Field

When you really think about it, the playing field is where all of the selling action is. If you control the playing field, you will win the sale. If someone else controls the playing field, he or she will win the sale. That is why all of your actions as a sales person should be devoted to controlling the playing field.

In Chapter 2, we listed a variety of tools that could help you in the business development process. These tools included a newsletter, press releases, public speaking, and technology such as the fax machine and the Internet. These tools now take on added significance in light of our playing field discussion.

These tools should be clearly used as business development tools. However, they should also be used as tools to help you set the playing field. In fact, everything you do as a professional sales person should be directed toward controlling the playing field. The more you can manage customer perceptions about what is important in a relationship, the more likely you will be successful in your sales career.

First to Customer

Unfortunately, setting the playing field takes time and the earlier you enter the sales cycle, the more likely you can set the playing field.

Figure 7-2 shows the three possible options for entering the sales cycle. You can enter the sales cycle *early* (if you are lucky), you can enter the sales cycle in the *middle* (as is most often the case), and you can enter it *late* (if you are unlucky).

If you enter the sales cycle late, you have very little opportunity to work with customer perceptions and set the playing field. You are likely going to be playing on someone else's playing field.

The playing field could have been set by the competition. In this case, that company has worked with the customer to determine

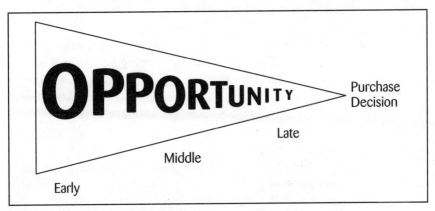

Figure 7-2. First to customer

what is important in a relationship. The competition's strengths or unique selling points will have a much greater chance of aligning with customer perceptions of what is important in a relationship and that company will likely win the sale.

Because you are so close to the point of sale, you will have very little opportunity to manage or mold customer perceptions and you will wind up competing on price. At the point of sale, this may be your weapon of last resort.

If you enter the sales cycle late, you could also be working on the customer's playing field. More often than not, the customer's playing field is going to be price. Customers have a tendency to view most vendors as purveyors of a commodity product or service, with the major defining characteristic in the transaction being price.

Customers do this because it is the easiest way for them to compare two or more competing organizations. Customers compare us on the basis of price because it may be the one apparent common denominator in two or more completely different product or service offerings. Finally, customers compare us on the basis of price because we don't offer them an alternative basis of comparison.

If you arrive late in the sales cycle, you will have only a limited opportunity to manage customer perceptions about what is important in a relationship. The playing field will have been set by someone else and your only position of merit will be to lower your price.

If you arrive in the middle of the sales cycle, you will have some ability to work with customer perceptions and help set the playing field. Unfortunately, the customer will also have had some time to either set its own perceptions or work with the competition to set its perceptions.

Here, we are in a better position than if we enter the playing field late. However, we are still going to have a tough go of it since we do not clearly control the playing field. We are just one of many on the playing field and while there will be some opportunity to differentiate our company, price will still be a major element in the decision-making process.

Enter the sales cycle early!

Since entering the sales cycle in the middle or entering the sales cycle late doesn't present us with viable options over the long run, the clear answer is to enter the sales cycle as early as possible. The earlier you enter the sales cycle, the more likely you are to have an impact on the playing field and, therefore, the more likely you are to win the sale.

The great learning point is that you have a choice as to when you enter the sales cycle. In the first sales cycle, where you enter the cycle is determined by chance as much as anything else. This is why I said if you enter the cycle early, you are lucky, and if you enter it late, you are unlucky.

However, once a sale takes place, a new sales cycle starts—and here is where you have a choice. You can always enter the new sales cycle at the beginning.

When we lose a sale, many of us sit around and lament our loss for 364 days and hope things will be different the next time around.

When we win a sale, many of us pat ourselves on the back for 364 days and expect to win the sale again.

This is not how the real pros would do it.

The real pros would understand the value of controlling the playing field and that is why they would do exactly the same thing—win, lose, or draw.

No matter what the outcome of the first sale, you goal should be the same—to control the playing field for the second sale.

If you won the first sale, you have 364 days to make certain you control the playing field for the next sale. If you lose the sale, you have the same 364 days to make certain that you control the playing field for the next sale.

Providing the Customer with Valid Alternatives

The final method of molding customer perceptions is to *provide the customer with valid alternatives.*

Creative options or valid alternatives are the essence of the red-hot sales process. In fact, earlier in this book we talked about Paul's Rule of One. There, we suggested that the sales person must not lose any time when there is only one option on the table.

The alternative is to provide the customers with many options to serve their needs. Again, this is the essence of the red-hot sales process.

The red-hot sales process can be best described as the process through which we add value in the sales cycle. The steps of the red-hot sales process are outlined below.

1. *Gather information* through your value audit.
2. *Analyze customer objectives* with your value-management question.
3. *Refine customer preferences* through the techniques presented in this chapter and throughout this book.
4. *Recommend a solution* that serves the needs of the customer. Remember that you will derive your success from the success of the customer.

You must constantly be working with the customer to develop a strategy or solution that will suit the customer's needs. By providing options all along the way, you never back yourself into a corner. More important, you are offering different and possibly unique solutions to the customer's needs.

Concluding the Purchasing Process

The final two steps in the purchasing process are to:

- Differentiate your offering.
- Create a perceived fit with the final buying criterion in comparison with the competition.

A major portion of this book has been devoted to how to differentiate your offering.

We started with the premise that great sales people differentiate themselves on the basis of the quality of their ideas.

Then we gave you a number of tools to help you in the differentiation process. Among these tools were the model for analyzing your customer's business, the six categories of value, the quantification methods, and the value audit.

Unless you can differentiate yourself in a competitive market, you will be in a commodity position. The only way to differentiate yourself when you are in a commodity position is on the basis of price.

The final step in the purchasing process is to create a perceived fit with your product or service and the final buying criterion. This was the purpose of your value audit worksheet.

The heart of the worksheet focused on the questions you would ask in your value audit. The questions were designed to uncover customer needs and position you for success with the account.

Opposite the questions in your value audit worksheet were your company's unique selling points. The purpose of placing the unique selling points here was to help you draw a parallel between the customer's needs and your strengths as an organization.

Conclusion

This chapter was devoted to the ultimate selling tool and the art of "setting the playing field." Setting the playing field is the essence of the sales process. The ultimate selling tool is one great way to set the playing field.

Setting the playing field is where we can have the greatest impact on our long-run success.

The next chapter will be devoted to our value basket. We are going to provide you with a tool that will facilitate the information-gathering process with your key accounts.

Chapter 8

Your Value Basket

here is one final ingredient to our success formula. This final ingredient is called your *value basket.*

Your value basket is the tool that we are going to propose to collect and gather data about your customers over time.

Your value basket will give you the opportunity to plan how to approach your accounts. Your value basket will give you the opportunity to develop strategies to penetrate your accounts. Your value basket will also give you the opportunity to differentiate yourself in a competitive market. Finally, your value basket will give you the opportunity to develop a value-based pricing strategy with your customers.

Where to Use Your Value Basket

As you will see, your value basket is a complex set of tools that you can use to improve your chances of success in the sales cycle. However, because your value basket is a complex set of tools that will require time and effort to implement, you may want to be selective about the accounts you choose to work with in this manner.

I recommend that you prepare and maintain a value basket for the top 10 accounts in your sales portfolio. Your top 10 accounts should be measured on the basis of current revenue.

160

In addition to maintaining a value basket for your top 10 accounts, you may want to consider maintaining a value basket for your top 10 prospects as well. Your top 10 prospects should be measured on the basis of future buying potential as described in Chapter 1.

The reason you also want to maintain a value basket for your top 10 prospects is because of what I call *continuity planning*.

Continuity planning tells us that one thing you can count on in sales is *change*. Companies are merging with other companies, companies are buying other companies, and companies are going into and out of business almost every day.

Given that customers are moving in and out of the market daily, you can never rest on your laurels as a sales professional. You must always be planning for your next large account. This is where continuity planning comes into play.

One of the best account managers I ever worked with had an uncanny ability to perform continuity planning. He knew that one of his large accounts would no longer be a large account one year from today through no fault of his own. Therefore, to remain a top producer, he knew he must always be planning to get his next large account.

For example, suppose that one of your top accounts merges with another company. Also suppose that the buyers for your product or service in the merged entity come from the company you were not working with prior to the merger. You would stand a great risk of losing this account. This is where continuity planning comes in.

Continuity planning tells you that your top accounts may no longer be top accounts a year from now. Therefore, it always pays to plan on where you are going to obtain your next large account.

It is crucial that you consider your top 10 prospects in addition to your top 10 accounts as you implement our value basket approach.

Your Value Basket

Your value basket is designed to help you maintain information about your customers over the long run. You can then use this information to add value into the customers' sales cycle and to improve your chances of success in the sales cycle.

The first section of your value basket is presented in Figure 8-1.

This section of the basket is designed to help you collect general information about your customer and is called the General Information section.

Company name _____

Account no. _____

Mailing address _____

_____

_____

Telephone _____

_____

Critical challenges facing this customer _____

_____

_____

_____

Fiscal year _____

When budgets are prepared _____

Vision statement (Attach copy if possible) _____

_____

_____

Customer's five-year sales plan _____

_____

_____

_____

Annual report obtained _____

Press releases or other general information obtained _____

Prepared by _____ **Date** _____

Figure 8-1. Value basket general information

The General Information Section

While the General Information section contains some basic information, such as company name, address, and phone number, this section starts to develop some very important issues that we have raised through out this book.

The first is the *critical challenges facing this customer*.

This entire book has been devoted to making your customers successful. A starting point for this success is to understand the critical issues facing their business.

Every business has obstacles it must overcome. In order to differentiate yourself in a competitive market, you must drive to the heart of the customer's business. This is the goal of this section of your value basket. If you can help the company overcome its difficulties, you will overcome your own in so doing.

There are two other extremely noteworthy points in the General Information section.

The first additional point we need to consider is the customer's *five-year sales plan* and *vision statement*.

The customer's five-year sales plan and vision statement pick up where the previous section about critical issues left off.

Critical issues typically speak to a customer's business *today*. A five-year sales plan and a vision statement, on the other hand, speak to a customer's *future* business.

In fact, these were the two points we were trying to make when we asked our value-penetration questions in Chapter 6.

The two value-penetration questions from our value audit were:

- Given what you are doing now, are there areas for improvement?
- What is your future direction?

It should not surprise you to see that the value audit developed in Chapter 6 and the value basket presented here are designed with the same goal in mind.

The purpose of the first value-penetration question was to find a niche selling opportunity. Remember that a niche selling opportunity is going to provide the customer with something that the company needs but does not have.

This is also the purpose of the critical issues section of the value basket. Here, we are trying to provide the customer with something that the company needs but does not have.

The second question about future direction was again designed to uncover a niche selling opportunity. This is also the purpose of understanding the customer's five-year sales plan and vision statement.

Both the five-year sales plan and the vision statement speak to where the customer is going. As you know, future business is, by definition, a niche selling opportunity since it is clearly something the customer needs but cannot possibly have already. These two segments of your value basket are also designed to position us for a niche sale.

Your Customer's Budget Cycle

There is one additional noteworthy point in the General Information section of your value basket. You should always be familiar with your customer's *budgeting process*. This is the time when most existing relationships are renewed and when new relationships are formed. This is the time when you will have either the opportunity to solidify your position as the incumbent provider or the opportunity to penetrate your competitors' accounts.

In Chapter 7 we talked about the value of being first to customer. There, we noted that the earlier we enter the sales cycle, the more likely we can manage customer perceptions about what is important in a relationship. We also noted that after a sale takes place, a new sales cycle starts.

Your customer's budget cycle will tell you when a new sales cycle starts. This is when existing relationships are renewed and new relationships are developed. Make certain that you are aware of the customer's budget cycle.

Your Overall Sales Goals

The next section of your value basket is entitled Overall Sales Goals. This section is presented in Figure 8-2.

This section of your value basket begins by listing your sales to the account for the prior three years. This information is used to create an annual forecast for this account for the current fiscal year.

When you consider your sales projection for an account for the current fiscal year, you should base your forecast on two factors.

First, your forecast should be based on the *historical trend* highlighted above. In other words, if our historical sales analysis indicates

---

Company name _____

Account no. _____

Account manager _____

Historical sales, prior three years

    FY 19___ _____

    FY 20___ _____

    FY 20___ _____

Projected sales, current fiscal year

    FY 19___ _____

Major business activity for current fiscal year

(Remember that your major business activity should support your sales projection for this year)

Project	Anticipated Volume	Date

Figure 8-2. Overall sales goals

that sales to this account are growing at a rate of 10% per year, it might be plausible to assume that they are going to continue to grow at this rate. Likewise, if sales have been declining with this account over the prior three years, it would be hard to argue that this year we anticipate a 25% increase unless there has been a significant change in the account relationship.

The second factor that we should consider when developing our sales forecast is the *major business events* for the customer this year that will likely result in business for our company.

If the customer is planning on opening four new offices in the current year, there may be significant sales opportunities with each new office opening. This event should be documented in our sales plan and also form the basis for our sales forecast for the current fiscal year.

Specific Sales Goals for This Year

Once we have developed our overall sales goals, we must get quite a bit more specific. How do you expect to achieve your goals? What are your specific sales goals for this account? Figure 8-3 is designed to help you develop your specific sales goals for this account.

Specific Sales Goals for This Year	
Description of Goal	**Date to Complete**
(Attach action plan)	

Figure 8-3. Sales goals worksheet

Assume that you had a goal to sell $500,000 of your services to this account this year. Assume that sales last year to this account were $400,000. You are projecting a 25% increase in sales. What specific goals do you have to set in order to achieve the overall sales goal of $500,000?

In this instance, your specific sales goals might appear as follows:

- *Goal #1:* Last year we sold $350,000 of existing services to this account. This year, we are going increase sales of existing services by 25% or $87,500. This would bring sales of existing services to $437,500.
- *Goal #2:* Last year we introduced a new service to the market. This customer showed some interest in the new service but we did not make a sale. This year, we are going to sell $62,500 of the new service to this customer.

As you can see, it is not enough for an account manager to say he or she wants to sell more this year than last. It is not enough for a sales person to identify a specific account and say he or she would like to penetrate the account identified.

While these goals are certainly pointing you in the right direction, they are not specific enough to give you the guidance and direction necessary to be successful.

In order to have meaning, your overall and specific sales goals must conform to what I call *The Seven Rules of Effective Goal Setting.*

The Seven Rules of Effective Goal Setting

Rule #1: Place your goals in writing. This is the first step in the goal-setting process. This is the purpose of your value basket.

Goals that are in writing tend to be realized. Goals that are not written tend to become compromised by reality.

Written goals cause you to focus. You become aware of things that you might not have otherwise noticed. All of your conscious and subconscious powers become focused on the goal and, as a result, your chances of achieving the goal are greatly enhanced.

On the other hand, goals that are not in writing have a tendency to be compromised by reality.

Assume that you set an annual sales goal of $1,000,000. This would imply that you should sell approximately $80,000 in a given month in order to attain your annual goal.

Let us also assume that you fail to put the goal in writing and half a year goes by. You check your actual progress to date and compare it with your half-year sales goal of $500,000. You notice that you are quite a bit short.

Suppose, for the sake of the example, that you have year-to-date sales of $300,000, not the $500,000 you were expecting. It is at this point that your original goal will begin to be compromised by reality.

Since you did not place your original sales goal in writing, you might not remember whether your original goal was $1,000,000 or $750,000. Since $750,000 is a more likely outcome at this point, you establish this as your new annual sales goal. In other words, your sales goal is beginning to be compromised by reality.

You might have to repeat this process at the end of the third and fourth quarters as well if it appears that you may be short of your revised goal.

Place your goals in writing and you will greatly enhance your chances of success in the sales cycle.

Rule #2: Make certain your goals are specific and measurable. Once you place your goals in writing, make sure they are specific and measurable. Sales goals such as "I want to sell more" or "I want to penetrate a certain account" are not sufficient for our needs.

Goals must be specific and measurable in order to be effective and motivating. If goals are not specific or measurable, you have no way of really knowing whether you have achieved them or not. Setting non-specific or non-measurable goals is not much different from not placing your goals in writing at all. You will have no real way of measuring your progress toward your goals and hence your goals will again tend to drift back toward reality.

Rule #3: Include a time element in all goals. Goals must also include a time element. The statement "I want to sell $100,000" takes on completely different meanings when we are talking about a day, a week, a month, a quarter, a year, or a decade!

Rule #4: Challenge and stretch. When setting goals, you should always challenge and stretch.

There is a great story in motivational literature that highlights the need to constantly challenge and stretch.

It's a story about a grasshopper that was placed in a glass container. Cellophane was placed over the top of the container so that the grasshopper could not jump out.

Since the grasshopper could not see the cellophane, it continued to try to jump out of the container. It would jump as high as it could, only to hit the cellophane ceiling and then fall back to the ground.

Soon, something began to happen.

The grasshopper began to jump to a level just below the cellophane. It stopped trying to get out. Even when the cellophane was removed, the grasshopper never tried to get out again.

When setting your goals, ask yourself, "Am I limiting my own potential?"

In sales, you must grow in order to prosper.

Growth requires that you challenge and stretch.

As you set your goals, reflect upon all of the unthinkable breakthroughs in sports that have occurred in recent memory: the four-minute mile barrier broken by Roger Bannister, Babe Ruth's all-time home run record broken by Hank Aaron, Roger Maris' single season home run record topped by both Mark McGwire and Sammy Sosa, and Lou Gehrig's consecutive game streak broken by Cal Ripken, Jr.

These were all thought to be barriers that could not be overcome.

I think it would be safe to assume that even the records set by Aaron, McGwire, and Ripken will also some day be broken.

The lesson to be learned here is that in order to be successful you must grow. If you are not growing, your competition probably is and whatever success you enjoy will be short-lived. Further, do not place limiting beliefs upon yourself. Sometimes, we can be our own worst enemy in this regard. That brings us to our next rule.

Rule #5: Believe in your ability. Now that you have your goals in place, you must believe in your ability to achieve them.

One of my customers is a group of Indian diamond merchants. They hired me to help them learn how to sell jewelry in the United States jewelry market.

On one of my trips to India, I had the opportunity to visit the house of Mohandas K. (Mahatma) Gandhi.

As you probably know, Gandhi was the great Indian leader who freed India from British rule.

As I toured Gandhi's house, I could still feel his presence in this house, even though he had been dead for many years.

As I stood there in awe of his accomplishments, my mind began to wander. After all, Gandhi was quite a sales professional. You could say that at the end of his career he had 950,000,000 customers. His customers were the Indian people, the people who followed his guidance and direction.

I began to wonder how one actually gains 950,000,000 customers. After all, Gandhi started out alone.

Martin Luther King, Jr., another great achiever, also started alone. Any president of a country starts out alone. And any great sales professional starts out alone.

As I stood in Gandhi's house, I began to wonder how somebody starts out alone and rises to a level of such great achievement.

The answer I came up with is that all high achievers have at least two things in common.

First, all high achievers have great ideas. Gandhi had great ideas. King had great ideas. And all top-performing sales professionals also have great ideas.

However, more important than their ideas is a firm belief that they can accomplish great things.

Gandhi had great ideas. But more important, he firmly believed in what he could accomplish. King also had great ideas. But again, he believed in his ideas so strongly that he was willing to give his life.

They both were able to attract and inspire millions of people and convince them of the importance and potential of their ideas.

Great sales professionals also believe in their ability to achieve their goals.

When you establish your sales goals, your goals are no different from the goals established by Gandhi or King. You may not be leading the multitudes, but your success depends on moving people and convincing them that you have something great that will improve their lives.

In order to do that and achieve your goals, you must believe in your ability to accomplish what you set out to do.

Rule #6: Be realistic. When setting your goals, you must challenge and stretch, but you must also be realistic. Goals that are unrealistic tend to be demoralizing. If you do not believe that you can succeed, you may stop trying. Make certain that your goals are challenging, but also make certain that they are realistic.

Rule #7: Evaluate your goals periodically. Finally, remember to evaluate your progress periodically. Goals are always based on assumptions, not on facts. You must constantly evaluate your goals to make certain that you are on the path to success.

The sales year consists of 52 weeks or 12 months or four quarters. Choose appropriate sales periods and set evaluation points. Use those points to assess your progress toward your goals. Do not wait until 11 months into your fiscal year to see if you are going to reach your goals. If you are off course, it is probably too late to make adjustments 11 months into the year.

Consider evaluating your goals periodically to make certain that you are on track. Remember that goals are based on assumptions and assumptions can turn out to be true or assumptions can require modification. If your assumptions require modification, make the appropriate adjustments in your day-to-day selling activities.

Your Action Plan for the Current Year

For each major account goal, there needs to be a plan in place to achieve the goal. This is the purpose of your action plan. Figure 8-4 shows a worksheet for managing your action plan for the current year.

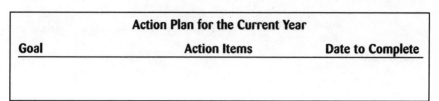

Figure 8-4. Action plan worksheet for the current year's goals

Your action plan is designed to document the specific steps you or your company needs to take in order to realize the specific sales goals of the prior section. For example, if one of your sales goals is to introduce $100,000 of your new product into the customer account by the end of the year, your action plan relating to this specific goal might be as follows:

- Perform a value audit to define the customer's needs. This should take place by the end of month 1.
- Have an internal meeting to discuss the implementation of the new product in the target account. This should take place by the end of month 2.
- Develop a proposal concerning the introduction of the product to the customer. This should take place by the end of month 3.
- Present proposal to the customer by the end of month 4.
- Incorporate customer feedback into the preliminary proposal by the end of month 5.
- Reposition proposal with customer and close the sale by the end of month 6.

It was Joel Barker who said, "Vision without action is merely a dream." If you set goals without developing a plan of action, you are just dreaming. "Action without vision is simply passing time." If you develop a plan without having a goal, you are just passing time. However, "vision with action can change the future." When you combine setting goals and planning, you can change the future.

What steps are you going to take to ensure your success?

The Key Decision-Making Groups

Key decision-making groups are another crucial element of your value basket. Who plays an influential role when the customer makes a buying decision? Figure 8-5 is designed to help you identify the buying influences as well as to develop a proposal that will be of value to each of the four buying influences.

	Know-how	Supply chain	Support	Ease	Strength	Design
Facilitator						
Certifier						
User						
Check signer						

Figure 8-5. Key decision-making groups for the customer

Robert B. Miller and Stephen E. Heiman, in their book *Strategic Selling*, introduced the concept of the different buying influences within an organization. Miller and Heiman told us that there are four buying influences within any organization:

- The facilitator
- The certifier
- The user
- The check signer

The significance of the four buying influences is threefold.

First, many sales people work with only one of the four buying influences, the facilitator. The facilitator is the influence within your customer who initiates the purchase transaction. More often than not, this will be a purchasing agent.

Working with only one of the four buying influences means that you could be very sensitive to staff turnover in that position.

If you are working with a purchasing agent and the purchasing agent leaves the company, the new purchasing agent may or may not keep you on as the primary provider of products and services to his or her company.

Remember that new brooms sweep clean. A new purchasing agent may come into the company with favorite providers or simply the desire to establish a presence by changing the status quo, which could include changing providers. By working with more than one buying influence within an organization, you reduce the risks inherent in staff turnover.

Second, by virtue of the fact that you may be working only with purchasing managers, you may notice that your sales cycles have an extremely heavy focus on price.

If you were to review the score card or appraisal format for purchasing managers, you would notice that much of their success is determined based on the price reductions they receive from companies like yours. Their job is to get you to lower your price.

As you will see, by working with the other buying influences within a company, you have the opportunity to diversify away the price issue.

While purchasing agents or purchasing managers have a clear price focus, the other buying influences do not. By working with the other influences in the sales cycle, you can diminish the impact of price on the overall sales process.

Finally, any of the four buying influences can say no to a sale. There is only one influence who can say yes. If you are not working with all four buying influences, you dramatically diminish your chances for a successful outcome.

The roles of each of the buying influences are discussed below.

The Facilitator

As discussed above, the facilitator influence is the influence within an organization that initiates the buying process. This is typically not the decision-maker, but rather the influence designated to gather the information required to make an informed purchase decision.

As you know, the facilitator influence typically has a great focus on price.

There are three strategies that I have found very useful in working with the facilitator influence. The goal of these strategies is to shift the facilitator away from the strong price focus.

First, integrate the four buying influences strategy into your basic selling approach. One question that I always ask in my face-to-face meetings with a customer is "Who else is involved in the decision-making process?" The goal of this question is to bring the other buying influences into the selling cycle.

The purchasing agent may be helpful and identify the other buying influences. However, the purchasing agent may also say that he or she is the sole decision-maker in the sale.

Before I tell you how I would respond when a purchasing agent is less than supportive, I must tell you that the four buying influences exist in every sale.

When you are working with a large corporation, each buying influence may be shared by more than one person at the customer. For example, suppose that you are working with a company that has two regions, the east and the west. The customer might have one representative from each region exercising buying influence. Therefore, you would have an "east" facilitator influence and a "west" facilitator influence. The same would be true of the other three buying influences. Here, the customer would involve eight people in the purchase transaction.

On the other hand, you may be working with either a small company or a department within a larger organization. Here, one person may actually play more than one role. However, the four buying influences would still exist!

Once, we were working with a department within AT&T. There were two people involved in the sales process. The first was the department head. He represented both the facilitator and check-signing influences. A training coordinator was also involved in the sale. She represented both the certifier and user influences. The four buying influences were present in the sale. However, in this instance, only two people represented them.

The same might be true if you were working with a smaller corporation. The four buying influences would still exist. However, they would typically be represented by fewer than four individuals.

The four buying influences exist in even the simplest of selling situations.

One of my customers is a company that sells college test preparation services. If you have a child in high school and you want to prepare your child to take the SATs (the college entrance examination), you might consider sending your child to my client for assistance.

This is a fairly simple selling situation in that the dollar amount of the sale is typically small and the customer usually takes the program only one time.

However, I was surprised to learn that the four buying influences exist even in this simple situation. Typically, one of the parents played the role of the facilitator. The second parent plays the role of the check signer. The student is obviously the user of the program. The school guidance counselor played the role of the technical certifier because he or she advised the student on the merits of the program.

As you can see, you are making a safe assumption when using a strategy based on the four buying influences with a customer account.

What if the facilitator does not cooperate?

There will be instances when a customer may try to block your implementation of the four buying influences strategy. Earlier we noted that a purchasing agent might claim to be the only one in the organization responsible for the purchase decision.

It is very common for a purchasing agent to respond in this manner. In fact, I would suggest that it might be the rule and not the exception.

What I do in this situation is build the four buying influences model into my selling approach. In fact, one of my unique selling points is designed to help me implement this important strategy.

I presented the unique selling points for my business in Chapter 2. Here they are again, for your convenience:

- *One-stop shopping.* In my business, I offer a full range of sales training programs, keynote speeches, and sales consulting services. This gives me the unique opportunity to serve all of your needs in the sales performance area. The key benefit to the customers is that they make a single purchase decision, as opposed to many, and that they get consistency of application throughout their programs.
- *Real-world expertise.* Whenever I go on a sales call, I always get asked what qualifies me to teach others how to sell. I believe the

answer to that question lies in three basic facts. One, I grew my first business from 0 to $100 million in sales in just 10 years. Two, since entering this business, I have had experience in most major industries and with market-leading organizations. Three, I practice what I teach; I also sell. Every single day that I am not delivering a program, I am either on the telephone setting up appointments with prospects or meeting with prospects face to face. Therefore, the solutions my customers receive in my programs work!

- *Performance Plan*™. Every program I deliver is customized to meet the needs of the specific customer. Our proprietary customization process is called the Performance Plan™. The Performance Plan™ was developed based on my 15-plus years in the training business and based on sound adult learning principles. The Plan combines the appropriate level of theory with practice and real-world expertise to maximize learning results.
- *Broad portfolio of offerings*. Within each of our three service lines—training, consulting, and keynote speeches—we provide a full and complete set of offerings. We offer seven fully customizable sales training programs, six keynote speeches for meetings and conferences covering the latest issues in the sales field, and a full range of consulting services, including our modular System for Selling Success™.
- *Value-based approach*. Out goal is not to deliver a sales training program, for example. Our goal is to have a tangible bottom-line impact on your business. After one recent program that I delivered, the sales manager said this was the best sales training program he had ever attended; but more important, he said this program would make his group a minimum of $8,000,000 in incremental sales.

Our third unique selling point, the Performance Plan™, is designed both to differentiate us in a competitive market and to allow us to implement the four buying influences selling strategy.

When I position our company for success with a customer, I always take the time to explain our approach to doing business. This approach is embodied in the Performance Plan™.

The Performance Plan™ is a proprietary approach to sales training that looks at the customer organization from a comprehensive perspective. I tell the customer that in order to implement this approach and maximize the company's return on investment with me, we will need to have access to others within the organization.

In other words, I answer the customer's question of "What's in it for us?" (i.e., maximum return on investment) if the company allows me to implement our proprietary approach to sales training. I also remove from the sales cycle the issue of who is responsible for the purchase decision.

Before we move on to our next point, I want to take the time to point out that your business can have a "performance plan" of its own. One of your five unique selling points should always be devoted to a proprietary business process, something that the customer can get only from you.

The competition can copy your ideas, but a customer that wants the real McCoy must come to you. You should take the time to brand your proprietary business process. Once you have done this, you will begin to create a proprietary market position for your company.

The second strategy I have found useful in working with purchasing agents is the one I presented in Chapter 7. There we discussed creating a list of the variables involved in a sales transaction:

- Price
- Payment terms
- Delivery
- Warranty
- Training
- Installation
- Length of agreement
- Volume of agreement
- Pre-payments
- Financing terms
- Customer support
- Other variables particular to your industry

You know that purchasing managers will typically raise price as a critical decision-making point in their sales cycle. Therefore, you must be prepared with a list of alternatives so that you can begin the negotiation process.

This is simply an application of Paul's Rule of One. You cannot position yourself in a sales cycle with only one variable involved in a sale.

I have found payment terms, length of agreement, and volume in the agreement to all be suitable alternatives to a price reduction.

Please note that I am not advocating that you reduce your price. One of the major points of this book was to help you maintain premium pricing in a competitive market.

However, there will be instances when all of the sales strategies that we have outlined will not deliver us to the position we desire with the customer. Price will enter into your sales cycle no matter how effective you are at selling. This is particularly true when you are working with purchasing agents.

Purchasing agents often get rated on their ability to get a lower price. So be prepared with a list of alternatives in the event that price arises in your sales cycle.

My favorite alternative is payment terms. In fact, when the customer asks me for a lower price, I try to negotiate for pre-payment of the entire contract. This will allow me to use the money for other investments for the duration of the contract.

Many larger businesses are willing to make large pre-payments. The reason they are willing to do this is because of their budget cycle.

For example, suppose one of your large accounts has budgeted $100,000 at the start of the fiscal year for your product or service. What matters, then, is how close the company can come to the budget amount, not the timing of the payments from the budget.

This means that the company may be willing to pre-pay for products and services in return for a reduced price. A reduced price will mean that the company finishes the year under budget. This will help the purchasing agent in his or her year-end evaluation.

Some customers are prohibited from making pre-payments. This is why you want to have your list of negotiating variables ranked in order of importance to you. If the first negotiating variable does not work with a customer, simply move on to the next. Length of contract and contract volume are also great alternatives for the sales professional, because they allow you to make up for reducing the price by reducing the costs of future sales and marketing.

The third great strategy I have developed for working with purchasing agents is to review the categories of value presented in

Chapter 4 and determine where I can develop a personal win for the purchasing agent:

- Business know-how
- Supply chain optimization
- Operational support
- Ease of doing business
- Organizational strength
- Product or service design

It is not a good idea to make generalizations in your quest to deliver value and differentiate yourself in a competitive market. However, I would suggest that when working with purchasing agents you are going to be more likely to find value of interest to them in the areas of business know-how and ease of doing business. Operational support and organizational strength might be a close second.

One of the interesting points about the Miller/Heiman model is that different buying influences will have different sources of value. That is, different buying influences will enter the sales cycle from a different perspective.

This means that we must become adept at tailoring our product or service offering depending on which of the buying influences we are working with.

Earlier in this book I told you the story of how we were able to save a large pharmaceutical company $2,000,000 in the cost of processing vendor invoices. What I didn't tell you was that the first time we presented the idea, the customer rejected the proposal.

Why? Because we did not do a good job of translating the proposal into a win for the purchasing agent. He told us that we had a great idea. However, the great idea, although it would save his company $2,000,000, would not impact his budget or his performance evaluation.

It was only when we were able to mold our proposal into something of value to the purchasing agent that we piqued his interest and won the sale.

Certifier

The second of the four buying influences is the certifier influence. The certifier influence is designated to evaluate the features and benefits of your product or service, to make certain that it meets the required specifications of the company and that it will perform up to expectations.

Sales people are also typically adept at working with the certifier influence. I would suggest that the average sales professional spends more time with the certifier influence than with any other influence except facilitator.

The certifier influence is crucial to your success as a sales professional since this influence helps you get your product specified. If your products are not specified with a customer organization, it will be very difficult for you to make a sale.

A great selling strategy to help you shift away from the price issue is to work with the certifier influence before you work with the facilitator influence. If you can get your product specified in enough depth before the purchasing function gets involved in the sale, it will be difficult for price to be a primary issue in the sales process.

For example, suppose you are selling widgets and your company has just developed a new feature, called feature X, that can improve customer productivity by 10%. You are the only company in the market with feature X. If you can get the certifier influence to specify that feature X must be included in all widget purchases made by the company, it will be difficult for the purchasing agent to make price a major decision point in the sale. Rather, the agent will be charged with the mandate to find widgets with feature X. These would be, of course, the widgets made by your company alone.

Getting your product specified by the certifier influence can have a major impact on your selling success. The ultimate selling tool that we developed in Chapter 7 is great for working with the certifier influence. In fact, the ultimate selling tool was designed to ensure that your product or service was uniquely specified at the customer account.

However, keep in mind that the ultimate selling tool was actually designed to have your product or service specified by all four buying influences within an organization. That is to say that the ultimate selling tool is intended to present your organization as a whole, not just from a product perspective.

You need to be careful when you are working on the basis of product alone. Much of the value you can deliver is on a non-product basis. Make certain when you are working to get your *product* specified that you are actually working to get your *company* specified. By including the non-product elements of your business, as well as the product elements, you greatly enhance your chances of success in the sales cycle.

User

The user influence is the third influence in the Miller/Heiman selling model. This influence is exercised by the people who will ultimately use your product or service.

If you are selling into a manufacturing environment, the user influence will likely be the people on the assembly line. If you are selling into a service environment, the user influence will be the people who use your service to improve their productivity.

Ease of use is the primary focus of the user influence, because the end users are the ones who will be using your product or service day in and day out.

The significance of the user influence is that these people can easily block your sale.

Imagine that you have done a great job with the certifier influence and a great job with the facilitator influence. You are well on your way to a sale. How likely are you to succeed if the end users in the company will not use your product or service if it is purchased?

The answer to the foregoing question is obvious. Make certain to include the user influence in your sales cycle as these people can also greatly enhance your chances of success.

Check Signer

The check-signer influence is the final influence in the Miller/Heiman model. This is, perhaps, the most important influence in the sales process.

The check-signing influence is the individual or group of individuals in the company with either budget or check-signing authority. This is the decision maker who can say yes to the sale.

Remember that any of the decision makers listed above can say no to a sale. This is the only one who can say yes.

The check-signing influence would tend to be the highest ranking of the four buying influences. Job titles such as CEO, Plant Manager, Department Head, and CFO would not be uncommon.

The check-signing influence is also the influence that would be most receptive to the messages developed in this book. They are the people within an organization who are focused on organizational success.

Unfortunately, this is also the influence that sales people are least likely to work with, because they might fear the potential rejection that could come from calling on this type of individual.

Earlier in this chapter I mentioned Mahatma Gandhi and his rise to greatness. I also mentioned Martin Luther King, Jr. and his rise to greatness. Well, I did this for a reason.

There, I told you that all great achievers start out alone and then, through great ideas and a strong conviction in their ideas, rise to greatness.

One of the messages that these stories send to me is that success can come from anywhere. Just like Gandhi and King rose to greatness, so can we! Therefore, we must always ask ourselves the question, "If somebody has to be great, why not let it be me?"

Before Gandhi became a great leader, he was just Mahatma Gandhi. Before King became a great leader, he was just Martin Luther King, Jr.

Now you might be wondering how this little pep talk relates to professional sales. The answer is simple.

In this section of the book, I have just asked you to call upon CEOs and other high-level executives within your customer. Most sales people would be afraid to do this. Their fear of rejection will prevent them from working at this level.

However, it is at this level that we will derive our greatest success. Therefore, we must make the effort.

My feeling is that some sales person out there is going to call on the CEO of your customer and actually be successful. Therefore, you have to start to ask yourself the question, "If someone is going to be successful in this regard, why not let it be me?"

One of my customers had an account manager who listened to my pep talk and made a cold call to a CEO of a major corporation. He was successful in securing the meeting and went on, over a period of years, to develop a substantial account relationship.

Make certain to identify the check-signing influence within your customer organization and make certain to include this influence as part of your sales efforts.

When working with CEOs and other high-level executives, also remember that their focus in a sales transaction will typically be quite different from those of the other influences listed above. They will be focused on return on investment rather than the other elements of a sales transaction.

In Chapter 5, we showed you how to quantify the impact of your ideas. There, we developed four methods of quantification. When working with CEOs, you must take your quantification analysis one step further.

How to Present Return on Investment

Before I show you how to present your product or service on the basis of return on investment, I want to go on record as stating that every, yes, every product or service can be presented in this manner.

Return on investment, simply stated, is "what you receive" divided by "what you pay."

If you were to invest $100 in a certificate of deposit at the beginning of the year, the $100 would represent what you pay. If you were to get $5 in interest over the course of the year, the $5 would represent what you receive. If you take the $5 (i.e., what you receive) and divide it by the $100 (i.e., what you pay), you get a 5% return on investment.

All too often, sales people focus on the "what you pay" element of their relationship with the customer. This is why most sales have such a strong price focus.

If you want to create red-hot customers, you must focus on the "what you receive" element. Chapter 5 of this book was devoted to showing customers what they receive. This was the whole purpose behind our quantifications.

Suppose that you are selling $100,000 of products or services to a customer during a particular year. The $100,000 would represent the sum total of your invoices to the customer. This is the "what you pay" element of the relationship.

Now suppose that you develop your quantifications as we proposed in Chapter 5. Let us assume that the total dollar value of your savings and incremental sales (at gross margin) was $200,000 for the year and the customer was supportive of these quantifications.

Before we calculate the customer's return on investment with us, there is one small modification that we must make to our approach.

Many of the products and services that we sell to the customer are consumables. This means that the customer does not have them at the end of the year. This is in contrast to our example of the certificate of deposit, where the customer still has the original $100 investment plus the $5 received in interest.

My service, sales training, would be a good example of a consumable service. After the sales training program, the customer no longer has the investment, but only the return on that investment.

If you are selling a consumable product or service, one that will be used up during the course of the year, you must deduct the cost of your product or service from the "what you receive" portion of the calculation.

In order to calculate the customer's return on investment in the example we provided, you would first have to take the $200,000 return the customer received and deduct the $100,000 the customer paid you for your product or service. The remaining $100,000 is the true "what you receive" in our example.

You then divide the $100,000 received by the $100,000 paid to calculate that the customer receives a 100% return on investment with you.

There are several noteworthy discussion points that we can develop as a result of our analysis.

First, remember that any product or service can be presented in this manner. All you have to do is perform the calculations and believe in the results.

Second, do not be alarmed at the magnitude of the customer savings. In this case, the customer saved twice what it spent with us.

When you become adept at the red-hot sales process that we have presented in this book, it is not uncommon to actually save customers more than they spend with you. This is particularly true when you consider that many of your ideas are cumulative. This means that the customer benefits actually continue from one year to the next.

The magnitude of the customer savings also leads us to two interesting points.

First, if we are saving the customer so much money, price should not be the major determining factor in a sale. The customer will always have a price focus until we show that price is only one element of a sales transaction.

Second, the magnitude of our savings also means that we may be significantly underpricing our products and services. If, for example, we are charging the customer $100,000 for our product and the competition would charge the customer $90,000 for a similar product, we have quite a bit of pricing flexibility. In fact, our pricing flexibility would approach $190,000. This is the figure that we get when we take the $200,000 savings we generated for the customer and subtract the $10,000 price differential.

How do I know if my return on investment is good?

In order to determine whether your return on investment will motivate the customer to action, you must look to the return that the customer is receiving on its other investments.

Companies measure their business activities in several ways. The key measures are the following:

- Return on investment
- Return on assets
- Return on equity
- Internal rate of return
- Internal hurdle rate

While there are differences in the way these items are calculated, you can use any one of the above measurements as a general measurement for the return the customer is receiving on its business investments.

When I refer to business investments, I am obviously referring to the investments a company makes in its property, plant, and equipment. I am also referring to the investments a company might make in the equities and debt of other organizations. Finally, I am referring as well to the investments customers make with companies like yours. The customer's overall return includes all of its investments, including the investments made with all of its suppliers.

Every purchase made by a customer is an investment of resources. Every purchase by a customer must be made to improve the customer's overall return on investment.

In order for you and the customer to know that your proposal is a good proposal, the return that you deliver must exceed the average return that the customer is receiving on the composite of its other investments.

For example, suppose that your customer is receiving an average return of 20% on its investments. If your proposal, offer, or product generates a return in excess of that rate, the customer should be very inclined to accept your proposal.

On the other hand, if your return does not exceed that rate of return, the customer may have better options than to work with you.

Your goal should be to develop a proposal that will help the customer increase the return on its investments.

You can learn about your customer's return on investment through two primary sources.

The easiest way to learn about your customer's return on investment is to ask. Often customers will be willing to share their internal hurdle rate in order to help you succeed as a sales professional.

If your customer is unwilling to share this information, you can often find out about return on investment through a review of the customer's annual report or other financial reports. If your customer is not a public company, you may consider using similar information from companies in their industry that are public companies. Finally, if no information of this nature is available, you can always use assumptions and business models as discussed in Chapter 5.

Final Thoughts on Key Decision-Making Groups

Identifying the key decision-making groups at your customer will greatly enhance your chances of success in the sales cycle. Remember that any of the key decision-making groups can say no, so it is imperative that you work with each influence in order to maximize your chances of winning the sale.

The foregoing discussion should also highlight the fact that each buying influence approaches the sales process from a different perspective. Figure 8-5 has been designed with this one thought in mind.

Not only do you want to identify your customer's key decision-making groups, you also want to think about what value you can bring to the sale for each of the key decision-making groups. This is why we have taken the six categories of value and used them as headings in our matrix.

As you identify your customer's buying influences, think about the particular elements of value that would be important to them, given their different roles in the customer's business.

Analysis of the Competition

Unfortunately, we do not operate in a vacuum. It would be nice if we did not have any competition. However, since we do, we must be aware of not only our strengths as an organization, but also our weaknesses relative to the competition for a particular account.

Remember that selling is the successful management of customer perceptions about what is important in a relationship. Therefore, you must become adept at raising the visibility of your strengths in the market.

You should also be aware of your competitors' strengths. After all, your competitors are going to be trying the raise the visibility of their strengths in the market.

Whoever is more successful at positioning their strengths will likely win the sale with a particular account.

There may also be external or environmental factors that enter into the equation. These external factors could include changes in the political or economic climate, new product introductions, or new technology introductions.

In order to track your competitive advantages, competitive disadvantages, external opportunities, and external threats as they relate to a particular account, we would like you to refer to Figure 8-6, "Analysis of the competition." Here's how it works:

- *Competitive advantages.* These are advantages that are internal to your organization that will typically produce positive sales results. Your unique selling points would clearly fall into this category (USP1-USP5).
- *Competitive disadvantages.* These disadvantages relate to the strengths of your competition. These would typically be your competitors' unique selling points (CUSP1-CUSP5). While I do not believe in speaking poorly of the competition, I do believe that you must be aware of their strengths in order to effectively compete in the market. Here is where you have the opportunity to document and strategize about your competitors' strengths.
- *External opportunities.* These are factors outside your company that could produce positive results for your organization with this account. These could include changes in the political climate, the economic climate, new product introductions by the customer, and new technology advances in the marketplace.

	Know-how	Supply chain	Support	Ease	Strength	Design
Competitive Advantages	USP 1	USP 2	USP 3	USP 4	USP 5	
Competitive Disadvantages	CUSP 5		CUSP 1	CUSP 2	CUSP 4	CUSP 3
External Opportunities						
External Threats						

Figure 8-6. Analysis of the competition

- *External threats.* These are factors outside your organization that could produce negative results for your company with the target client account. These would take the same form as those outlined above for external opportunities.

As you can see from a review of Figure 8-6, we have not only taken the time to analyze our competition, but we have also placed our analysis in the context of the value-creation model we developed in Chapter 4.

Unfortunately, your competitors may also be adept at bringing value to the market. Thus far in this book, we have discussed value creation only as something that you bring to the market.

Since the competition may also be doing things to create and deliver value to the customer, you not only need to understand your competitors' strengths as organizations, but also to understand them from the perspective of the bottom-line impact they may have on the target account.

For example, suppose that your invoice price exceeds that of the competition by $10,000. This is the price differential that you believe you must justify.

However, suppose that a competitor also delivers $15,000 of non-product value to the account as part of its proposal or offering. If you ignore the $15,000 of non-product value, you may underestimate the value you need to include with your offer in order to win the account.

The foregoing discussion was meant to demonstrate that competition must factor into your value analysis. It was not meant to imply that you should deliver only enough value to just win the sale.

Your value delivery should be commensurate with the potential rewards at the account. The larger the account potential, the more value you should be prepared to deliver. Further, given the account potential, you should be prepared to deliver sufficient value to guarantee the sale. Remember that Paul's Rule of One tells us to diversify away our risk of losing the sale by bringing numerous value opportunities to your customer's sales cycle.

Completing Your Value Basket

There are several additional steps that are required in order to complete your value basket. These additional steps are outlined below:

- New products, services, or strategies to be introduced into the account this year
- Your pricing strategy
- Your team selling plan

Planning New Product, Service, or Strategy Introductions

The account development cycle presented in Chapter 6 gave us a good indication of the direction we should be taking with a particular account. It spoke strongly toward growing the account relationship and included moving progressively from small sales to larger sales to exclusive providership.

As you develop your account relationship, you must think about the new products, services, or strategies that are required to grow the account relationship. The word "relationship" implies long-term planning and here is where you get to develop your long-term plan for new product, service, or strategy introductions.

Your product, service, or strategy introduction plan should start with the potential value ideas that we developed in Chapter 4. Here again, we have presented the six categories of value.

However, we cannot deliver value in a vacuum. Value has meaning only in the context of the customer's business. It is for this reason that we have taken the six categories of value and shown you how they may work with the five elements of a customer's business.

Remember that any idea presented to a customer should be presented from the perspective of improving the company's bottom line. Figure 8-7 was designed with this goal in mind.

Planning Your Pricing Strategy

As we all know, the issue of price is bound to come up in most selling situations. Remember also that we are preparing our value baskets for our larger accounts and larger potential accounts. Because the potential business volume with this type of account will tend to be substantial, the issue of price will take on even more significance.

Figure 8-8 (page 192) is designed to help you plan your pricing strategy with the account. Figure 8-8 reflects the discussion that we first developed in Chapter 5. Here, we are going to begin the process of quantifying the impact of our recommendations.

Our chart begins by comparing the invoice price of your product or service with that of the competition. Then we must add and subtract the value elements of the equation to arrive at the true cost of doing business for the customer. In other words, this section of your value basket is designed to help you and the customer understand the difference between *price* and *lowest total cost solution*.

Please note that when you add and subtract the value elements of the equation, you should be including not only the value elements that you bring to the customer, but also the value elements that you believe the competition brings to the customer. This was discussed in the competitive analysis section above.

Planning Your Team Selling Plan

The final element of your value basket is presented in Figure 8-9 (page 193). This element of your value basket is entitled "Account

	Receipt	Manufac-turing	Shipment	Sales	Service
Know-how					
Supply chain					
Support					
Ease					
Strength					
Design					

Figure 8-7. New products, services, or strategies to be introduced into the account

Team Analysis." The account team analysis has been provided for two reasons.

First, many of the value ideas that you bring to your customers will require support from others within your organization. For example, earlier in the book I told you about a time when our accounting staff was required to work with the customer accounting staff in order to reduce the customer payment cycle from 90 days to five business days. Our accounting staff would be part of the account

Product 1	Our company	The Competition
Invoice price		
Value idea 1		
Value idea 2		
Value idea 3		
Competition's first value idea		
Competition's second value idea		
True cost		

Product 2	Our company	The Competition
Invoice price		
Value idea 1		
Value idea 2		
Value idea 3		
Competition's first value idea		
Competition's second value idea		
True cost		

Product 3	Our company	The Competition
Invoice price		
Value idea 1		
Value idea 2		
Value idea 3		
Competition's first value idea		
Competition's second value idea		
True cost		

Figure 8-8. Pricing strategy

team for this business transaction. The Account Team Analysis section of your value basket allows you to document which people within your company are responsible for different elements of the account relationship.

Second, we went to great lengths within this chapter to impress upon you the importance of the four buying influences. If the customer has more than one party involved in the sales transaction, you may want to have more than one party on your side as well.

When you think about developing your account team, remember that there are two types of account teams.

Account Name		
Account Number		

Our Personnel	Responsible for contacting...	Frequency

Prepared by _____ **Date** _____

Figure 8-9. Account team analysis

First, there is the *relationship* team. The relationship team is responsible for ongoing account development. Members of the relationship team typically come from the sales function, since they have ongoing responsibility for developing long-term relationships.

Second, there is what I call the *value* team. The value team includes any members of your company who are responsible for helping to bring a specific element of value to this customer account.

Make certain to include both relationship team members and value team members in your Account Team Analysis.

Conclusion

This chapter presented our value basket. It should come as no surprise to you that the value basket is simply one element of an account planning process. I did not want to present a complete account planning process to you, since many sales professionals would already have an account planning process in place.

Rather, I chose to present the value basket because it took the ideas and strategies presented earlier in this book and delivered them to you in a manner that could easily work with your existing account planning process.

The value basket was designed to easily supplement your existing planning process.

The final chapter of this book is going to be devoted to account maximization. There, we are going to present six easy-to-implement strategies that you can use to get and keep red-hot customers for life!

Chapter 9

Conclusion: Account Maximization Strategies

This book has been devoted to making your customers red-hot. It is my firm belief that you can be successful in sales only if you first make your customers successful.

Chapters 1 and 2 of this book were devoted to taking your message to market. There, we taught you how to define your target market so as to maximize the return you receive on the time you invest in the sales cycle.

Chapters 1 and 2 were also devoted to giving you strategies to motivate prospects (i.e., those that have not purchased from you) to take the first step and buy from you. This is a formidable challenge, since customers and prospects are always trying to mitigate their risk of doing business with a new supplier.

Finally, Chapters 1 and 2 pointed out that we will likely be more successful if we follow a large account strategy.

Chapters 3 through 8 were devoted to showing you how to penetrate the large accounts in your sales portfolio.

Your selling success is going to be a function of your ability to penetrate the larger accounts in your sales portfolio. In other words, your selling success is going to be a function of your ability to maximize the value of the accounts you have.

This is not to imply that prospecting and business development have no place in today's sales environment. They most certainly do.

However, once you make your first small sale to an account, you will likely be better off fully penetrating this account than finding a new one to penetrate.

I want to conclude this book by providing you with what I call the six principles of account maximization.

These principles are taken from the strategies presented in this book and summarized here to give you six clear-cut steps that you can take to immediately improve your sales results.

The six principles of account maximization were developed from my first business, where we had between 300 and 400 account managers. All account managers were ranked according to sales performance.

Over the years, we noticed that three or four account managers were always at the top of the list. The order among the top performers would change from year to year. However, no other account manager was able to penetrate the top tier of account managers.

We began to study the top performers in our business to learn what it was that they were doing in common.

The first thing that we learned was that they were applying the tools and strategies outlined in this book. The second thing that we learned is that we were able to summarize their strategies into six easy-to-implement ideas—the Six Principles of Account Maximization.

The Six Principles of Account Maximization

The six principles of account maximization will help you create large accounts in your sales portfolio. (Remember that a large account is one with both consistent and significant revenue.)

The six principles of account maximization are discussed below.

Principle #1: Know Your Customer's Business

The first principle of account maximization is to know your customer's business. In fact, this was the focus of Chapter 3, where we talked about extreme customer focus.

There we developed a structured process for analyzing your customer. The process was based on a model first developed by Michael Porter. The model told us that every customer business has five distinct business segments. The business segments presented in Chapter 3 were:

- The receipt of inbound shipments of raw materials
- The manufacturing process
- The shipping of finished goods to customers
- The marketing and sale of finished goods to customers
- The service of finished goods for customers

In addition to understanding your customers' business, it is important to understand the market within which they operate. Instead of trying to sell your products or services, you must position yourself to make your customers more successful.

This requires that you not only understand how their products or services perform in the market, but also how the customers position themselves as organizations in the market.

Every company, whether its representatives are aware of it or not, has both a red-hot cause and unique selling points. Make certain to fully understand both for your customer. Also make certain to document your understanding in the value basket presented in Chapter 8.

Remember that the goal of your sales effort is to make your customer more successful. And success is defined in terms of business results. Information is the most powerful ally you have in this regard and a strong understanding of your customer's business, its entire business, should be a fundamental element of your information-gathering process.

Principle #2: Become Part of the Organization

Becoming part of the customer organization is one of my favorite account maximization principles. It is both easy to implement and powerful in application.

I first learned about this principle when working with one of the four top-performing account managers discussed above.

I can remember spending a day in the field with the account manager and going to customers to perform what I always considered to be routine tasks. For example, he would take the time to drop off information instead of mailing it. He would always personally deliver urgent information instead of using an overnight delivery service. Finally, when in an area, he would always stop in and see his customers and prospects.

At every appointment, delivery, or casual meeting, he would always say the same thing: "Isn't it great to see the face behind the voice?" He was becoming part of the customer organization.

This account manager would become so entrenched with his customers that they often gave him a company badge so that he could move freely within their facility and make use of their company cafeterias. He had a whole supply of corporate badges in his desk drawer for going from customer to customer.

One day, this account manager asked me to go on a sales call with him.

The meeting was with Banker's Trust.

Banker's Trust has two main locations in New York City, one downtown in the financial district and one in midtown Manhattan.

We were the exclusive provider of computer training for the downtown location. And true to form, this account manager had a Banker's Trust badge for use at the downtown location.

We had never done business with the midtown location. However, the account manager was successful in securing an appointment. He, of course, wore his Banker's Trust badge.

I was so surprised when the meeting began. There were only limited introductions and no discovery (i.e., that portion of a meeting devoted to understanding the customer's needs). We went right to the end of the meeting and started closing sales.

The customer had seen our Banker's Trust badge and just started placing an order. The customer representative asked for the corporate rate and gave us the units and dates of delivery that the branch required. That was it! The meeting was over. In five minutes we moved from first sale to exclusive provider.

Why?

Because we had a badge.

It might surprise you to know that we had no corporate agreement with Banker's Trust. All we had was a badge. However, because we appeared to be part of their organization, any barriers to our success seemed to be immediately removed.

It is great to see the face behind the voice. Take every opportunity to integrate your company into the operations of the customer account. This is what we were talking about when we told you about the last step in the account development cycle—proactive account management. Here, you have done such a great job with the customer account that you have fully integrated your business into the customer's business.

Principle #3: Become a Consultant

Becoming a consultant was the focus of Chapters 4, 5, and 6 of this book.

In Chapter 4 we developed the potential product. The potential product was the actual product or service delivered by your company and all of the value you could layer onto the product or service.

There, we discussed the six sources of value:

- Business know-how
- Supply chain optimization
- Operational support
- Ease of doing business
- Organizational strength
- Product or service design

In Chapter 5, we developed a process for showing the customers that the value we delivered had a tangible, bottom-line impact on their business. Remember that the bottom line in business today is success. We must be adept at showing the customers how our products, services, and ideas improve their business results.

Finally, in Chapter 6, we gave you a process—the value audit—that showed you how to integrate our red-hot selling strategies into your day-to-day business activities.

Today's business environment is extremely fast-moving and extremely competitive. If you want to be perceived by your customers as more than a peddler of commodity products and services, you must make red-hot selling a way of life.

Principle #4: Create a Good Operational Process

One of the six sources of value presented in this book was "ease of doing business." When I presented this idea, I told you about a survey that we did in my computer training business. The survey pointed out that ease of doing business was very high on the list of vendor selection criteria for many purchasing agents.

Creating a good operational process falls into the category of ease of doing business. This can be a tremendous source of value for the customer and something that is very easy for the sales professional to implement.

When you develop a new customer relationship, take the time to make certain that the transaction-processing elements of your business relationship are in order.

- Do you know who to send your invoices to at the customer?
- Does the customer know where to send the checks to your company?
- Can electronic funds transfers make invoice processing more efficient for both companies?
- Is all the information required by the customer present on your invoices?
- Is it easy for the customer to place orders?
- Is it easy for the customer to receive technical services?
- Do you return all customer phone calls within one business day?
- What else can you do to make the relationship more effective for both parties?

These are all questions you need to ask in order to create a strong operational process.

Remember the story I told you about a company that we were working with where we were able to reduce the length of time it took to receive payments from 90 days to five days. That representative told us the company would never leave us because of the strong operational process we had developed.

Too often we are too excited about the sale to develop a strong operational process. We leave this to chance. Also, our motivation is to sell more, not to develop a strong operational process.

Your greatest success in sales will come from further penetrating your current accounts and a strong operational process is one of the fundamental building blocks for a strong account relationship.

Principle #5: Work the Account at All Levels

In Chapter 8 we talked about the four buying influences within an organization:

- The facilitator
- The certifier

- The user
- The check signer

The four buying influences examine the customer organization from what I would call a *horizontal* perspective. That is, we are looking at the organization from a *cross-functional* perspective.

Working the account at all levels suggests not only that we develop contacts with the customer outside of the purchasing function. Working the account at all levels suggests also that we examine the customer and develop relationships at all levels within a function as well.

Get to know the department vice presidents and departmental secretaries in addition to your traditional contacts.

Today's vice president may be tomorrow's CEO. Today's departmental secretary might be tomorrow's vice president.

Develop grass-roots support for your products or services. Remember that a *yes* can come from only one influence within the organization. However, a *no* can come from anywhere.

Principle #6: Leverage Your Relationships

This is the final element of your account maximization strategy. Make certain to leverage your relationships.

One of the account managers for my computer training company was perhaps the best I had ever seen in this regard. He had taken the United Nations account, an account that we had given to him from a prior account manager, and was able to leverage that single relationship into 14 separate worldwide agreements with other related areas within the United Nations.

This account manager was one of our top account managers nationwide. He could manage the largest of relationships and rarely, if ever, needed support on a sales call.

One day he was calling on a major insurance company in New York and asked me to go along. I did.

The call actually turned out to be an extremely small opportunity. I wondered why he needed my help. After all, he really didn't need my support, or the support of anyone else, on any sales call he went on.

When we were leaving the company, I asked why he needed my support.

He turned around and pointed to the company name on the building. He told me that this was one of the largest insurance companies in the world. He said it was true that this was a small sale. However, it was his first opportunity with the account and he wanted to make certain that everything went well.

He told me that if he were to make that first small sale he would be able to leverage his small success to become the company's exclusive provider over the course of one year.

Needless to say, that is exactly what happened.

Take your successes in one department within a company and use them to create successes in other areas within the company. Also, don't forget to consider your customer's parent company, subsidiaries, joint ventures, and other related parties. There is really no limit to the extent to which you can leverage your success.

Conclusion

This book has been devoted to making your *customers* red-hot. This book has also been devoted to making your *sales career* red-hot.

We have shown you how to take prospects and make them into customers. We have also shown you how to take your customers and turn them into large accounts.

Two of the critical tools that we used in this regard were our ability to differentiate ourselves in a competitive market and our ability to add value to our customers' sales cycle.

I hope I have helped you define a new way to sell. The level of competition is fierce and I see it only increasing over the next two decades.

In addition, I see the use of technology entering into the sales process in an even greater way than it does now. Today, you can purchase many products and services through the Internet without the interaction of a sales professional. This trend is only going to increase over the next 20 years, again pushing our products and services toward the commodity end of the spectrum.

I believe that the last sustainable competitive advantage in sales is your intellect and your ability to make your customers more successful. The purpose of this book was to show you how to create red-hot customers through the use of your intellect and your ability to have a tangible, bottom-line impact on your customers' business.

Your intellect is the one thing that will never change. Irrespective of the competitive nature of the market, irrespective of the use of technology, and irrespective of any other environmental factor that may evolve, we will still have our ability to think and to use this knowledge to benefit both our customers and ourselves.

I want to wish you the best of luck and...

May your sales career be RED-HOT!

Index

A

Account development cycle
  account penetration expansion, 125-26
  customer needs and, 118
  exclusive provider, 124-25
  large sales, 122-23
  Paul's Rule of One, 118
  positioning company, 118
  proactive management, xiv-xvii, 126
  small sales, 119-21
Account managers, 6-8, 27, 30-31
Account maximization
  consultant, becoming, 199
  customer's business, 47, 66-71, 102, 196-97
  operational process, creating, 199-200
  organization, becoming part of, 197-99
  relationships, leveraging, 201-2
  work the account at all levels, 200-201
Account team analysis, 190-94
"All" approach, 11
Application knowledge, 47-48
Articles for magazines, 34
Assumptions method of quantifying value, 97-105

B

Balance sheet analysis, 73-74
Banner concept, 20-21
Barker, Joel, 171
Basic company knowledge, 47
"Best practices," 48
Book publishing, 35
Business development
  articles for magazines, 34
  book publishing and, 35
  cold calling for, 32
  consistency and quality, not urgency, 34
  customer focus and, 40
  electronic mail for, 37
  fax broadcasts for, 36-37
  fear of rejection, 4, 9, 14, 39
  focus on areas for impact and, 40-41
  marketing plan and, 38
  newsletters for, 33-35
  playing field, setting, 155
  press releases for, 35-36
  public speaking for, 36
  red-hot cause and, 38-39
  strategy, 24, 25
  telephone sales for, 32
  test for, 38-41
  unique selling points, 32-41
  Web sites for, 37-38

205